How to Form a Company

How to Form a Company

Dennis Roberts

B.Sc. (Econ.), FCIS

 ICSA Publishing

Published by ICSA Publishing Ltd
16 Park Crescent
London W1N 4AH

Typeset in 9.5pt Stone
by Special Edition Pre-press Services, London

Printed and bound in Great Britain by
TJ International Ltd, Padstow, Cornwall

British Library Cataloguing in Publication Data

A catalogue record for this book is available from the British Library

ISBN 1 86072 100 1

Contents

Draft Wordings

Preface

This book aims to bring within one cover all that is relevant to the formation of a private limited company. However, it does not stop with the issue of the Certificate of Incorporation; it includes also the steps needed to prepare the company for starting its business, such as choosing an accounting reference date, printing letterheads and other stationery and VAT registration.

With the help of this book a company can be formed within five working days at a cost of £20 – plus an hour or so at a computer. Clear, simple documentation can be prepared, which states from the outset the purpose of the company, the shareholders who will own it and the directors who will run it. Anyone inspecting the file at Companies House will gain an impression of competence – that things have been got right first time – instead of implied confusion when a ready-made, 'off the shelf' company needs to have almost everything changed before it is ready to commence business.

It is still quite common to form a company with just one or two nominees, each of whom undertakes, by signing the Memorandum of Association, to take and pay for just one share. It is perfectly legal for a company to start business with an issued share capital of just £1.00, but that would hardly inspire confidence in those with whom the company hopes to deal! Increasing the share capital usually entails a general meeting to empower the increase, followed by a board meeting to receive applications and allot shares. A return of allotments must then be filed at Companies House.

One of the advantages of preparing the documents 'in house' is that these complications can be avoided. All that is necessary is that the persons (individuals or companies) who are to be shareholders should sign the Memorandum of Association as subscribers, showing against their names the full number of shares they are to hold. They are then bound, from the moment the company is incorporated, to take up and pay for the number of shares written against their names. No formal allotment of shares is required and no return of allotments needs to be filed, though it is usual to record the facts at the first board meeting before issuing share certificates.

Company formation is a task that, sooner or later, will face many professional people – chartered secretaries, accountants or solicitors. They will have the theoretical knowledge and may well know the practical requirements, but, for the first time at least, will need the help and guidance without which the task may seem daunting. With the aid of this book, however, they should be able to proceed with confidence. Accordingly I have aimed:

1 to record all procedures so that none need be forgotten;
2 to provide draft forms of all documents to save time and speed preparation;
3 to express all this – drafts as well as explanation – in language as simple as possible, consistent with the need for legal certainty;
4 to record the draft documentation on a CD-ROM in a form that will speed the process of preparing timetables and documents for registration.

We are here concerned only with private companies, including guarantee companies, not with the plc – the public limited company. That said, I have tried to be comprehensive and to bring together all that is relevant for our purpose, much of which has hitherto been available only by reference to a number of separate statutes or reference manuals. I have covered the law (whether statute law, secondary legislation or decisions of the courts) to the extent that is necessary, but I have not made this in any sense another legal textbook; rather, it represents the accumulation and distillation of my many years of practical day-by-day experience as company secretary and as director of numerous companies, public and private. I have aimed to pass on my experience and to show not just how to form a company but also how one can safely adopt short cuts or time-saving steps (and where it would be unwise to do so). Unlike other guides on company formation, this book indicates the steps that need to be taken after the company is formed to prepare it for running its business.

Throughout this book references to 'The Act' are to the Companies Act 1985 as amended by the Companies Act 1989, unless the contrary is clearly indicated.

Although the book relates mainly to private companies limited by shares, most of it is equally valid for companies limited by guarantee. Significant differences are clearly indicated, but references to 'shareholders' should, for a guarantee company, be taken as references to members, and references to 'shares' should be ignored. Much applies also to companies without limited liability, although these are subject to additional regulation that is beyond the scope of this book.

I have tried to avoid personal pronouns, lest any take offence. Where it has been unavoidable I have written 'he' not from prejudice but to avoid the awkward pedantic styles so often associated with attempts to appear neutral.

Acknowledgements

Extracts from the Companies Acts and secondary legislation (including Table A and the prescribed company forms shown in Checklist C) are Crown copyright and are reproduced by permission of the Controller of Her Majesty's Stationery Office.

Dennis Roberts

How to Use this Book

What sort of company?

There are more than one million companies registered in the United Kingdom, and of these fewer than 2,500 are public companies, 'listed' on the Stock Exchange. Most of the others are, in effect, sole traders or partnerships that have been formed into companies to achieve limited liability for the proprietors or to ensure perpetual succession or to secure more favourable tax treatment. There are also subsidiaries, often wholly owned, which have been registered to differentiate a separate line of business or to provide (or protect) a trading name, and charities where incorporation (usually as companies limited by guarantee) simplifies administration – for example, in holding investments.

It is with these private, non-listed companies – the vast majority – that this book is concerned. Although much of the book may be relevant for the public limited company, 'listing' involves additional requirements that are not covered here.

Preliminaries – taking instructions

The need to form a new company can arise in various ways. A person in professional practice may receive instructions from a client or may have taken the initiative by advising incorporation for tax reasons or to secure other advantages. A professional in employment may receive instructions from the board or from the managing director to form a new subsidiary or to establish a consortium company. In all cases it is necessary first to consider the objective of the undertaking – not just the formation of another company but also its commercial or administrative purpose – and then to keep it constantly in mind as work proceeds. By so doing it should prove possible to work through this book chapter by chapter, adapting drafts or modifying procedural details to suit, and end up with a company that is not just ready to commence business but is also ideally suited for its specific purpose. This is one of the strongest reasons for doing the work 'in house' rather than passing it to others.

Why do it yourself?

Why bother to form your own company? Would it not be easier and quicker to buy a ready-made, 'off-the-shelf' company from a firm of company registration agents?

The standard, ready-made 'shelf' company may have its uses, but company formation is now so much simpler and quicker than it used to be that the advantages 'shelf' companies may have had in earlier years have disappeared. Even when the ready-made company is chosen with care, it will usually need to change its name, its directors and its secretary, and it may also need amendments to some of its Articles and possibly to the objects clause in its Memorandum of Association. It will still be necessary to hold a first board meeting before the company can commence business, to choose the accounting reference date most suitable for its particular business and to design stationery, including letterheads and invoices. Even if a 'shelf' company is chosen, much of this book will still be found useful.

But rather than putting up with messy, amended documents that may not really fit the case and could prove a stumbling-point for those unfamiliar with the background, a far better option is surely to prepare and file in the first place documents that really suit your special needs. It should take no longer to start with a blank sheet of paper and work through this book than to prepare all the documentation necessary to adapt a generalised product.

What of the other alternative: handing the whole job over to a firm of solicitors? This has obvious advantages for those unversed in such matters, but care will be needed with the instructions that are given. Perusal of this book should help. Nothing will be gained, however, if the solicitors merely provide a standard, ready-made company and offer to adapt it to your needs or even expect you to take it in unamended form. If you want a proper job done, with documents drafted to suit the circumstances, then the reminders, specimen wordings and drafts to be found in this book will help the solicitors as well as you and will speed and simplify the work.

Who should attend to the documentation?

It should be well within the competence of every qualified practitioner, whether a chartered secretary, chartered accountant or solicitor, to attend to the incorporation of a limited company. However, although the work is not difficult, it can be daunting the first time, even for the well qualified. Many separate aspects have to be brought together, often under time pressures, and some tasks cannot be started until others are completed. There are pitfalls to be avoided, but there are some short cuts that may safely be taken to save time and money. Even the qualified and experienced will value checklists and draft wordings embodied in a practical working manual, with drafts ready to be downloaded from a CD-ROM.

Whereas the qualified should be able, with the aid of this book, to do with confidence all that is necessary, from the company's inception to the point where it is ready to start business, the uninitiated should proceed with caution. There is more to company law and secretarial practice than will be found between these covers. A final check on the documentation just before registration may be prudent, and if most of the work has already been done, professional advice should not prove expensive. Auditors or lawyers can provide such advice, but the professional whose speciality lies in this field is, of course, the chartered secretary. A list of chartered secretaries in public practice who form companies and provide related services is available from the Institute of Chartered Secretaries and Administrators (see page 154)

Even the professional who is well qualified in one discipline may on occasion need to consult others, and cases where this is desirable are indicated in the text.

How to use this book

The book is self-explanatory and the chapters have been arranged in logical sequence so that all the work may be carried out in the best and most convenient order.

The first step, after reading through the Table of Contents, should be to make working copies of Checklists A and B: 'Company Formation' and 'Taking Instructions to Form a Company'. These can be photocopied from the book or printed out from the CD-ROM. You should then read the book chapter by chapter, copying or downloading the draft documents as required and editing them to your own purposes. If at any point you are held up – waiting, perhaps, for stationery or for forms from Companies House – do not hesitate to move on. Although each chapter is self-contained with respect to its subject matter, the work covered in one tends to overlap with that in the next. However, this should not present any problems if you work from Checklist A.

Text documents on the CD-ROM can be downloaded and read by most common word processing packages, and the Companies House forms can be viewed and printed using the Acrobat reader supplied.

For more details on using the CD-ROM please visit our website, www.icsapublishing.co.uk

Forming a Company

1 An Overview

General principles

Company formation is not an objective in itself. The work needs at every stage to be related to the trading activities or other purposes for which the company is being formed and to the special requirements of the shareholders.

Even where speed is essential, the priority may be not so much to rush a batch of papers to Companies House as to design a letterhead that will 'sell' the company or its products or to register for VAT. Such points (which are seldom attended to by solicitors and other consultants) are built into the programmes and checklists described here.

What has to be done?

The principal components of the work involved in forming a company, from its conception to the commencement of its business, may be summarised thus:

1 Take instructions.
2 Prepare and file the documents at Companies House.
3 Attend to other business requirements, such as stationery, a bank account and VAT.
4 Await the Certificate of Incorporation.
5 Hold the first board meeting.
6 Prepare the various statutory books and records.

A moment's reflection will show that you cannot wait until one task is complete before starting the next. Work at one stage is apt to overlap, to affect and to be affected by others. If the work is not done in the right order, delay may result. Worst of all, some vital step may be forgotten. For all these reasons a little time spent at the outset preparing a detailed timetable, which will also serve as a checklist to ensure no detail is overlooked, will be amply repaid by the time saved or errors avoided as the work progresses.

Timetable

A timetable setting out the steps required to incorporate a new company up to the point where it is ready to commence business will be found in Checklist A. This can be photocopied or copied from the CD-ROM as a basis for your own timetable.

The Registrar of Companies aims to incorporate a new company and to issue the Certificate of Incorporation within five working days of receiving the relevant documentation. In an emergency, same-day registration is possible – at an extra fee. However, time must be allowed for preparing all the documents, collecting signatures and such commercial aspects as designing and printing letterheads and opening a bank account. Assume that the work, from start to finish, will take two or three weeks (possibly longer) before the company is ready to commence business. The purpose of the company may dictate not only the degree of urgency of the tasks but also the order in which they are tackled. For example, the critical factor before a trading company can commence business may be the availability of well-designed stationery, especially letterheads and invoices. If design consultants are to undertake this work, they may take far longer than the legal formalities. It may therefore be sensible to ask them to start preparing proofs even before it is known whether the company name will be available. By contrast, a company whose trade will be retail sales may need little or no stationery; for it, the urgency may lie in opening a bank account or in registering for VAT. For this type of company, printed stationery of adequate quality could be produced by computer as required.

Taking instructions: information required

When the timetable has been established, it is necessary to assemble the information required for incorporation. For the practitioner incorporating a family business, much of the information may be obvious, and writing it down may require no more than half an hour's conference with the client. For the secretary of a busy industrial group struggling to incorporate a new subsidiary, gathering the information may prove a long-drawn-out process. For example, the directors may know the purpose of the new company and have chosen its name but not be able to agree on the board of directors and other details, causing considerable delay. It is advisable, therefore, to ask for all the information required as early as possible. Checklist B, which may be copied as a reminder when taking instructions, sets out the information required.

When the information has been collated it is advisable to send copies to the instructing parties for checking and to send extracts to anyone else who needs to comment. For example, if proposed pre-emption terms (see Chapter 5) are to operate on the basis of an auditors' valuation, the auditors should obviously be consulted. They will doubtless need to know the basis on which they are to make their valuation and to ensure that there are unambiguous instructions in the shareholders' agreement or the Articles of Association.

Beyond the Companies Acts

Since the apparent objective is to form a company, it would seem natural to concentrate on the legal formalities and set other tasks aside. However, if the real objective is to have a company that is ready to start business, other matters beyond the Companies Acts and registration procedures must be set in hand at an early stage so that they may progress at the same time. The principal such items for most companies will be letterheads and other stationery, banking and VAT registration. For certain companies or businesses, other registrations (for example, with government departments or trade associations) may be necessary, and trademarks (or user agreements) may have to be prepared and registered.

All these matters should be included in the timetable so that they may be attended to at an early stage or referred to the appropriate specialist to progress alongside the company formation itself.

Letterheads and stationery are dealt with in Chapter 11. An early decision must be taken on various questions. What stationery is required? Should design consultants be employed or would it be sufficient simply to ask a reliable printer to prepare proofs? Will bulk supplies be ordered or will the stationery be run off on the office computer as required? Bulk printing should wait until the company receives its Certificate of Incorporation – since until then there can be no certainty over the company name – but meanwhile there may be advantages in having specimens produced early so that consideration can be given not just to the legal aspects but to the likely impression the stationery will give to a customer or supplier. Once the Certificate of Incorporation is received the stationery may be required urgently.

The procedure for opening a bank account is dealt with in Chapter 9, but at this stage it would be useful to tell the bank manager what is proposed and to ask for the necessary forms. These will include a draft of the board resolution on the authority of which the bank will open the account.

A general guide to VAT registration, with application forms, is available free of charge from the local office of HM Customs and Excise. A company cannot be formally registered for VAT until it has been incorporated, but delay can be minimised by prior discussion with the local VAT office (see the Directory at the end of this book or consult your local telephone directory under 'Customs and Excise'). Until a VAT number has been allocated it may not be possible to print certain stationery, particularly invoices.

Documents to be filed

To incorporate the company it will be necessary to file with the Registrar of Companies:

* The Memorandum and Articles of Association;
* Prescribed forms 10, 12 and (probably) 225;
* the registration fee of £20.00.

The Memorandum and Articles can be prepared (and subsequently photocopied) on plain paper; guidance is given in Chapters 3 and 4. The prescribed forms are reproduced (at reduced size) in Checklist C. The registration fee can be paid by credit card or by a cheque payable to 'Companies House'.

Prescribed forms

The Companies Acts require that certain information be filed at Companies House 'in the prescribed form'. These forms are prescribed by the Companies (Forms) Regulations 1985, as amended, and each form bears a number that corresponds to the section of the Companies Act 1985 by which it is required. Thus, section 363 requires an annual return, for which Form 363 must be used, and section 288(a) requires particulars of an additional director to be filed on Form 288a.

The forms required on or soon after the formation of a new company are the following:

* Form 10   Statement of first directors and secretary and intended location of registered office. If there are more than two directors, Form 10 (continuation) will also be required. Alternatively, a second copy of Form 10 may be used, with the relevant parts of pages 2 and 3 completed.
* Form 12   Statutory declaration of compliance.
* Form 225   Change of accounting reference date.

These forms, with notes on their completion, can be obtained free of charge from the Registrar of Companies. When forming a new company, ask for an incorporation pack, which comprises Forms 10 and 12 with 'Notes for Guidance'. The pack does not include Form 225 (to choose an accounting reference date other than the last day of the month of incorporation), so it is best to ask for this too when you ask for the incorporation pack.

The forms can be obtained by calling at any of the Companies House addresses shown in the Directory or may be ordered by telephone or e-mail. Blank forms can also be downloaded from the Companies House website or printed from the CD-ROM included with this book. In this case, a good quality printer is essential if the forms are to be acceptable to the Registrar of Companies (see Chapter 8 for more details).

Note that there is no 'prescribed form' for the Memorandum or Articles of Association. They must be typed in black on A4 paper. See Chapters 3, 4 and 8 for further information.

Most of the forms require several signatures and should therefore be prepared at an early stage. Advice on the actual completion of the forms and the procedure for filing them will be found in Chapter 8. Form 10 has space for only two directors, but continuation sheets are available on request.

Form 12, the statutory declaration that all formalities required by the Act have been complied with, must be completed last. It must not be dated earlier than any of the other documents.

The Registrar of Companies will retain the forms sent for filing. Photocopies, complete with signatures, should be kept for the company's own files.

Shareholders' agreement

Unless all the shares will be held by one individual, whether a holding company or a person, consideration should be given to whether, in addition to the documents required to form the company, an agreement between the shareholders – or at least between the principal shareholders – would be useful. The clauses that such an agreement might include are considered in detail in Chapter 5, but the question of whether such an agreement is necessary (or at least desirable) needs to be considered at the outset. Some of the provisions suggested in Chapter 5 could appear either in a shareholders' agreement, which is confidential, or in the Articles of Association, which are open to public inspection. This, too, could be considered at an early stage.

Merit in brevity

It is a popular misconception that legal documents need to be verbose.

The best lawyers – and the most effective documents – are often, in fact, the briefest.

Many 'outside' practitioners use standard wordings which, because they are drawn up to meet the needs of any business and every client, are of quite inordinate length and unnecessary obscurity. The Companies Act 1989 sought to end the verbosity so often seen in the objects clause in the Memorandum of Association, and although the message has not been accepted wholeheartedly, it is increasingly recognised that there is merit rather than danger in economy of words. At the same time, care must be taken to include all that is necessary. The specimen wordings in this book aim to achieve the best compromise between verbosity and insufficiency. Clauses that cannot safely be omitted are indicated.

If, however, the wordings in this book do not meet special require-ments – an unusual share pre-emption clause, for example, or special arrangements for appointing directors – it may be necessary to consider seeking specialist legal advice.

Ready to commence business

Shortly after the documents have been filed and the fees paid, a Certificate of Incorporation showing the new company's name and date of incorporation will be received. The new company may then safely have letterheads and other stationery printed (see Chapter 11) and hold its first board meeting (Chapter 9). Later board meetings may be con-cerned primarily with commercial and business matters, but the pur-pose of the first meeting is mainly to round off outstanding points arising from the incorporation, such as appointing officers, opening a bank account and issuing share certificates. It is therefore best to hold the first board meeting at the earliest opportunity.

As soon as possible after the meeting the statutory registers (register of members, register of directors, etc.) should be opened. Chapter 10 is devoted to this aspect, and specimen layouts for the registers will be found in Draft Wordings 9, 10 and 13.

What if something has to be changed?

The object of this book is to help those who are forming a company to avoid errors or omissions in the first place. But directors or shareholders can change their minds, or a company may develop in a way that was not envisaged at the outset. Chapter 12 has therefore been included to show the simplest ways of changing the formal constitution of a com-pany; and the same procedures can be followed to redress any errors or omissions that do arise.

If the information originally filed with the Registrar of Companies changes, the new data have to be filed. The procedure for making the change is explained in detail in Chapter 12. For any alteration to the name of the company, the Articles of Association or the objects clause of the Memorandum of Association, there is no prescribed form; a copy of the actual resolution must be filed, laid out in proper form as illustrated in Draft Wording 18. The forms most likely to be required for other changes are:

- Form 288a   Appointment of a director or secretary;
- Form 288b   Resignation of a director or secretary;
- Form 288c   Change of particulars for a director or secretary;
- Form 88(2)   Return of allotments of shares.

To transfer shares from one shareholder to another (or to a new shareholder) requires a Stock Transfer Form. This cannot be obtained from Companies House but may be purchased at any law stationers (find your nearest in *Yellow Pages* under 'Law Stationers' or 'Legal Stationers').

To sum up

Take instructions; make sure you have all the information you require; contact Companies House for the forms you need; photocopy (or print from the CD-ROM) the timetable in Checklist A. You will then be well on the way to forming your company.

2 Company Name

The name of a company, under section 26 of the Act:

1 must not be the same as the name of an existing company that appears on the 'Index of Company Names' kept by the Registrar under section 714 of the Act (this index includes not only companies registered in England and Wales but also those registered in Scotland or in Northern Ireland, as well as Industrial and Provident Societies, registered limited partnerships and overseas companies registered in the United Kingdom);
2 must not include any word(s) specified in an order made under section 29 of the Act, unless the Secretary of State approves;
3 must not give the impression that the company is connected in any way with HM Government or with any local authority in England, Wales or Scotland;
4 must not include, except at the end of the name, the words 'limited', 'unlimited', 'public limited company' or their abbreviations or Welsh equivalents;
5 must not be offensive;
6 must not amount to a criminal offence.

'The same name'

Requirements 4, 5 and 6 above are self-explanatory and unlikely to give rise to any difficulty. With regard to the first requirement, in determining whether two names are the same, words such as 'the', 'company', 'and company' and their Welsh equivalents are ignored, as are capital letters, punctuation and spaces. Note that this may produce some unexpected results. For example, 'H & S Ltd' or 'H. and S. Ltd' would be regarded as the same as 'Hands Ltd'. For this purpose too, 'Limited', 'Ltd', 'Public Limited Company' and 'PLC' or 'plc' are all disregarded, so you would not be permitted to register 'Hands Ltd' if there were already a 'Hands plc'. Similarly, 'Ltd', 'plc', and so on are regarded as the same as their Welsh equivalents.

The availability of names can be checked at any branch of Companies House or by phoning Cardiff (029 2038 8588) or Edinburgh

(0131 535 5800). Alternatively, you can check from the Companies House website (click on 'Free Information', where instructions will be found). In essence, you input the name you wish to use and Companies House will reply with a short list of the names most nearly matching. If your name is already there, you must choose another.

Prohibition is against a name that is the same or virtually the same. If your first choice is already in use, it should not prove difficult to devise a name that, although similar, is sufficiently distinctive. For example, if there is already a company called 'Smith Builders Limited' in the north of England, which constructs factories, you could choose 'Smith House-builders Limited' or 'Smith Builders (Southampton) Limited'. You should, however, use this ploy with care. If the name you choose is confusingly similar, you may be able to register the company, but the existing company could object within one year after the new company is registered on the grounds that the name, even though it is not the same, is so similar that customers might be confused. If the objection is upheld you could be required to change your new company's name. This in itself is not expensive, but it could be troublesome, especially if stationery has to be reprinted (or over-printed) and the name outside places of business has to be changed. You could also lose income.

Another danger is that an established concern may be able to bring a passing-off action and claim damages if it can show that it had lost custom or suffered other detriment to its business. However, this is a risk that every business runs, whether incorporated as a company or not, and it is usually possible to avoid trouble by ensuring that the name is sufficiently distinctive.

'Sensitive' words

The Appendix at the end of this chapter lists the words and expressions specified under section 29 of the Act for which approval is required from the Secretary of State. It is probably best to avoid these 'sensitive' words altogether. However, if you feel you have good reason, there is no reason why you should not apply for permission to include them. You should apply to Companies House, stating the name you wish to use and setting out your justification for the use of the word(s) in question. In certain cases, Companies House will require the application to be supported by written evidence that a 'relevant body' will not object to the proposed name.

The orders under section 29(1) of the Act list the words under various headings, making reference difficult and liable to error. To simplify searches the same words and expressions are listed in the Appendix in alphabetical order. Each word or expression is given one of five codes (B, L, N, R or S) to indicate the reasons why there may be objections to its use – and hence the argument you have to counter to present a strong case. The codes are explained in the Appendix.

If you decide to apply for approval to use one of these words you should obviously do so at the earliest opportunity. In the case of a word designated 'R' or 'L', write first to the body or government department named against the word, asking whether it has any objection. Then attach the reply to the application that you send to the Registrar of Companies with the other registration documents. Even in cases where a letter of authorisation is not essential, it will give added support to your application.

You should aim to present as strong a case as possible at the outset. It is suggested that the application (whether the preliminary enquiry to the relevant body or the eventual application to Companies House) should include:

1 the proposed company name in full;
2 a formal request to use the name that includes the specified word or words;
3 the reasons that you believe justify the use of the word or words (which may require an explanation of the nature of the proposed business or other activities, the company's size or pre-eminence, the intended location or geographical scope of its activities, the technical or professional qualifications of the directors, or similar relevant details);
4 any relevant history or precedent (in the case of a subsidiary company or a company reconstruction, for example, a similar name may have been in use for many years without giving offence or causing confusion, in which case this should be mentioned);
5 in certain cases, a supporting letter from the appropriate trade association, professional institute or local Chamber of Commerce (which, although not an essential prerequisite, may give added weight to the application);
6 where the word(s) in question is protected by legislation other than the Companies Acts, evidence that the legislation will not be contravened (as improper use would constitute a criminal offence).

Although Companies House will check the proposed name against its own index, it will not check against the register of trademarks. It would be advisable, particularly if the proposed name includes a 'made-up' word, to avoid infringing someone else's trademark by making a search at the Patent Office (see Directory for details).

A private company limited by shares and many guarantee companies must have 'Limited' (or its Welsh equivalent 'Cyfyngedig') as the last word in its name – and the word 'limited' must not otherwise form part of the name.

A company limited by guarantee may be granted exemption from including 'Limited' in its name, provided it satisfies the following conditions. First, its objects must be the promotion of commerce, art, science, education, religion, charity or any profession. Second, its Memorandum or Articles must require that all of its profits or other income be applied in promoting those objects, must prohibit the payment of dividends and must require that all its assets on a winding up be transferred to another body with similar objects. To claim the exemption, a statutory declaration on Form 30(5) must be sent to the Companies House with the other registration documents.

Although Companies House ignores minor differences in punctuation, such as hyphens, spaces or the use of capitals rather than lowercase letters, for business purposes it is better to be consistent. When the actual words of the name have been decided, it is a good idea to consider the exact form in which those words will appear:

- Which letters are to be capitals?
- What punctuation (hyphens, parentheses, commas, etc.), if any, will be used?
- Will the name include an initial 'The'? (Better avoided for brevity.)
- If 'and' is included, will it be spelt out in full or appear as '&'?

When these points have been resolved, the wording and style should be used consistently in all documents, not just those presented for filing but also those which form part of the company's stationery, including cheques and invoices, throughout the life of the company.

Appendix – 'Sensitive' words and expressions

The list below presents those words and expressions whose use in a company's name requires formal permission. In the list below,

N indicates a word that implies national or international pre-eminence.

B indicates that the word implies business pre-eminence or representative or authoritative status. In these cases you need to justify your application not only by reference to the size and scope of the company's intended activities but also by showing that the company can expect to be truly regarded as pre-eminent in the field implied.

S denotes words that imply specific objects or functions.

R indicates that an application to use the word must be supported by the 'relevant body' named in the right-hand column of the table.

L indicates that use of the word is protected by specific legislation. The relevant Act of Parliament is indicated. Misuse could be a criminal offence. In some of these cases there is a similar procedure to the 'R' names – application can be made to a relevant body, but reference should be made to the legislation for details, which differ from case to case.

Word or expression	Code	Relevant body or legislation
Abortion	R	Department of Health, Area 423
Anzac	L	Anzac Act 1916
Apothecary	R	The Worshipful Company of Apothecaries of London *Scotland:* The Royal Pharmaceutical Society of Great Britain
Architect	L	Architects Registration Act 1938
Association	B	
Assurance	S	
Assurance Broker	L	Insurance Brokers (Registration) Act 1977
Assurer	S	
Authority	B	
Bank, Banker, Banking	L	Banking Act 1987
Benevolent	S	
Board	B	

British	N	
Building Society	L	Building Society Act 1986
Chamber of Commerce	S	
Chamber of Trade/Industry	S	
Charity, Charitable	R	Charity Commission *Scotland:* Inland Revenue, Claims Branch
Charter, Chartered	S	
Chemist	S	
Chemist, Chemistry	L	Medicines Act 1968
Contact Lens	R	General Optical Council
Co-operative	S	
Council	B	
Credit Union	L	Credit Union Act 1979
Dental, Dentistry	R	General Dental Council
Dentist, Dental Surgeon/ Practitioner	L	Dentist Act 1984
Deposit	L	Banking Act 1987
Drug, Druggist	L	Medicines Act 1968
Duke	R	(As for 'Royal')
England, English	N	
European	N	
Federation	B	
Foundation	S	
Friendly Society	S	
Fund	S	
Geneva Cross	L	Geneva Conventions Act 1957
Great Britain	N	
Group	S	
Health Centre	R	Solicitor, Department of Health and Social Security
Health Service	R	NHS Management Executive, Department of Health
Health Visitor	R	(As for 'Nurse')
His/Her Majesty	R	(As for 'Royal')
Holding	S	

CHAPTER 2

Industrial and Provident Society	S	
Institute, Institution	B	
Institute of Laryngology/ Otology/Urology/ Orthopaedics	L	University College London Act 1988
Insurance	S	
Insurance Broker	L	Insurance Brokers (Registration) Act 1977
Insurer	S	
International	N	
Ireland	N	
Irish	N	
King	R	(As for 'Royal')
Midwife, Midwifery	R	(As for 'Nurse')
National	N	
Nurse, Nursing	R	United Kingdom Central Council for Nursing, Midwifery and Health Visiting
Olympic	L	Olympic Symbol etc. (Protection) Act 1955 (also protects variations, e.g. 'Olympiad' and Olympic symbol of five interlocking rings)
Optician, Optometrist	L	Opticians Act 1989
Patent, Patentee	S	
Patent Agent/Office	L	Copyright, Designs and Patents Act 1988
Pharmaceutical, Pharmaceutist, Pharmacist, Pharmacy	L	Medicines Act 1968
Police	R	Home Office, Police Department Strategy Group *Scotland:* Scottish Home and Health Department, Police Division
Post Office	S	
Pregnancy	R	Department of Health, Area 423
Prince, Princess	R	(As for 'Royal')
Queen	R	(As for 'Royal')

Reassurance, Reasurer	S	
Red Cross/Crescent/Lion and Sun	L	Geneva Conventions Act 1957
Register, Registered	S	
Reinsurance/Reassurance Broker	L	Insurance Brokers (Registration) Act 1977
Registered ...	L	Professions Supplementary to Medicine Act 1960 (Protects such terms as 'Registered Chiropodist', 'Registered Radiographer', etc.)
Re-insurance, Re-insurer	S	
Royal, Royale, Royalty	R	Home Office, 'A' Division *Scotland:* Scottish Office, Edinburgh *Wales:* Welsh Office, Cardiff
Scotland, Scottish	N	
Sheffield	S	
Society	B	
Special School	R	Department for Education and Employment, Schools 2 Branch
State ...	L	Professions Supplementary to Medicine Act 1960 (Protects such terms as 'State Chiropodist', 'State Radiographer', etc.)
Stock Exchange	S	
Termination	R	Department of Health, Area 423
Trade Union	S	
Trust	S	
United Kingdom	N	
University	R	Privy Council Office
Veterinary Surgeon, Vet	L	Veterinary Surgeons Act 1966
Wales, Welsh	N	
Windsor	R	(As for 'Royal')

3 Memorandum of Association

The constitution of a company is set out in two documents: the Memorandum of Association and the Articles of Association. The Memorandum sets out the formal structure of the company as seen by the outside world. The Articles regulate the company's internal affairs, the relationship between the company and its shareholders, its directors and its other officers.

The Memorandum must follow the style set out in Table B in the Schedule to the Companies (Tables A to F) Regulations 1985. There is no need, and indeed little opportunity, to depart from that style, illustrated in Draft Wordings 1 and 2. This basic draft should be varied only to the minimum extent necessary to fit the specific company. By copying what is required and inserting names, dates, etc., in appropriate places, a first draft may be prepared for approval and signature.

Information required

The Memorandum invariably comprises:
- *Clause 1* – stating the name of the company;
- *Clause 2* – stating whether the registered office is in England (or England and Wales) or in Scotland;
- *Clause 3* – the objects clause;
- *Clause 4* – stating that liability is limited (assuming this is so);
- *Clause 5* – stating the amount of the share capital and its division into shares or, in the case of a guarantee company, the intended number of members and the amount each member undertakes to contribute if the company is wound up;
- The *subscription clause*, which is not numbered.

Name (clause 1)

The choice of name for the company is fully covered in Chapter 2.

Registered office (clause 2)

The registered office of a company is the address to which all formal communications will be addressed. In the Memorandum of Association it is not necessary to set out the precise address of the registered office, only the country in which the registered office will be situated. If it is desired later to change the registered office, minimum formality is required (and no change in the Memorandum) provided both old and new addresses are in the same country, but it is virtually impossible to change the registered office from Scotland to England or vice versa.

If the registered office will be in Wales – or in England and Wales – the documents for registration must be sent to the Registrar of Companies in Cardiff. If in Scotland, they must be sent to Edinburgh. (For addresses, see the Directory.)

If the registered office will be in Wales, the Memorandum can state either that the registered office will be in Wales or that it will be in England and Wales. For most purposes the effect is the same, but there is one point on which the difference is significant. If it is desired to write some or all of the formal documents in Welsh, the Memorandum must state that the registered office is in Wales. In this case a statement that the registered office will be in England and Wales is insufficient. Subject to this point, a company whose Memorandum states that the registered office will be in Wales may use the Welsh equivalent 'Cyfyngedig' instead of 'Limited' as the last word of its name. Indeed, it can file the whole of its Memorandum and Articles in Welsh, but as it must then also file an English translation, notarially certified, this will rarely be seen as an advantage.

Objects clause (clause 3)

The objects clause states, in very general terms, the type(s) of business the company will be permitted to conduct. Prior to the Companies Act 1989, objects clauses were often very verbose because it was important to include every activity the company was ever likely to undertake, and there could be undesirable consequences if a company attempted to carry on some activity not covered by its objects clause. Thus the objects clause would refer not only to the intended business but also to similar businesses into which the company might expand at some future date. In addition, it would refer to such ancillary activities as borrowing money, paying pensions or acquiring other businesses and, in consequence, could become very lengthy. However, the Companies Act 1989 removed any limitations on a company's powers that might otherwise be inferred from its objects clause, and section 110 inserted a new sub-clause in the Companies Act 1985 which provides:

3A Where the company's Memorandum states that the

object of the company is to carry on business as a
general commercial company –

(a) the object of the company is to carry on any trade
or business whatsoever, and

(b) the company has power to do all such things as
are incidental or conducive to the carrying on of
any trade or business.

The intention was to avoid any restriction on a company's activities.
The objects clause can now be very brief, and drafting it no longer presents the problems with which it was once associated. The company
can now conduct any business or other activity that an individual could
carry on. For a trading company, the objects clause could state simply:

3 The object of the company is to carry on business as a
general commercial company.

But what if the company is not to carry on any trade or business at
all but, say, to act as a trustee or to operate a charity? It can be argued
that the wording of the Act, quoted above, is still adequate, but the pro-
moters may prefer something more specific – especially if the company
is not intended to make a profit. In this case it should prove easy
(bearing in mind that a company's activities are not restricted by its
objects clause) to draft a short clause that gives a clear indication of the
intended activities. A selection of such clauses (some of which have
been taken directly from Table B, mentioned earlier) will be found in
Draft Wording 3.

This leaves two questions. The first of these concerns loans.
Borrowing money is clearly part of a company's business and should
pose no problems. Lending money is arguably different: if the loan is
unrelated to the company's business, can it be 'incidental or conducive'
to its business? In practice, no problems are likely to arise, but there
may be difficulties if the company wishes to *guarantee some other company's borrowing* and perhaps give security for its liabilities. This problem can arise from a group arrangement to pool banking facilities.

For example, where a company is part of a group, a bank may provide
overdraft facilities to any and every company in the group on the basis
that every company will guarantee every overdraft – its own and that of
every other company in the group. Clearly, this could mean that one
company's guarantee is supporting another company's overdraft.
Several well-known banks, having taken legal advice, take the view that
such a guarantee is not part of the guaranteeing company's business
and therefore cannot be 'incidental or conducive' to that business. The

banks accordingly expect to see, spelled out as part of the objects of the company, specific power to give such guarantees and to give security in support of those guarantees.

It can be argued that the banks are wrong, legal advice notwithstanding, but it is easier and cheaper to concede than to pursue the point. A suitable wording, acceptable to most banks, could read:

> **3** The objects of the company are:
> **3.1** to carry on business as a general commercial company.
> **3.2** to lend money to and guarantee or indemnify the obligations and contracts of any other person or company whatsoever and to give security for any such loans, guarantees or indemnities.

In law the word 'person' includes a company, which is an artificial person created by the law, so it is not really necessary to write 'person or company'. Writing it out in full, however, prevents misunderstanding. The alternative sometimes seen – to 'guarantee or indemnify the obligations of customers and others' – is better avoided as the law would construe 'customers and others' as meaning 'customers and other persons in a trading relationship similar to customers'; this is precisely the interpretation we want to avoid!

The second question is whether shareholders wish to use the Memorandum to limit the discretion of the directors. For example, they may be prepared to invest their money in house-building but not want to run the greater risks they imagine could arise from building factories. Although this can be encompassed by drafting an objects clause that restricts the company to house-building only, its enforceability is open to question, and in any case it is usually better, with a small private company, to set out any intended restriction in a separate shareholders' agreement. The merits of this are discussed in Chapter 5.

A further point to note, particularly by those familiar with earlier practice, is that there is no longer any advantage in referring to the business of another company to be taken over. At one time this could reduce liability for stamp duty and capital duty, but these concessions were eliminated when the rates of duty were substantially reduced a few years ago so are no longer relevant.

For most of the companies with which this book is concerned, especially family businesses and wholly-owned subsidiaries where the interests of shareholders and directors are virtually identical, brevity and an objects clause drawn up in the widest possible terms have clear advantages.

Limited liability (clause 4)

For a limited liability company the wording of this clause is never varied. The following wording covers both a company limited by shares and a company limited by guarantee.

> **4** The liability of the members is limited.

A company where the liability of the members is unlimited can omit clause 4 completely (taking care to renumber what would otherwise be clause 5), since there is no requirement to state unlimited liability. In practice, however, clause 4 is often included in such cases, stating that members' liability is unlimited. Omission of the clause could prove a trap for those unversed in the finer points of company law; moreover, a statement that liability is unlimited can be a strong 'selling point' with the company's creditors. There is also the rather special case of the professions. Not all codes of professional conduct allow a professional practice to be conducted by a company, but even where they do there is often a rule that the professionally qualified members of the company shall carry unlimited liability. If the liability of all the members is to be unlimited clause 4 can read:

> **4** The liability of the members is unlimited.

If there are two types of member, one group providing the professional expertise and the other providing working capital, it may be necessary to divide the shares into two classes, in which case clause 4 could read:

> **4** The liability of holders of A shares is limited but the liability of holders of B shares shall be unlimited.

Share capital and its division into shares (clause 5)

The wording in Draft Wordings 1 and 2 will be self-explanatory. Clause 5 need not indicate whether the shares form a single class or are divided into several classes. This is better left to the Articles, where details of voting, dividend and other rights of each class of share can be set out in full. However, if different classes have different nominal values, these must be indicated in the Memorandum, e.g. ' ... divided into one thousand shares of one pound each and a further ten thousand shares of twenty-five pence each'.

Shares must have a nominal value, but it is not necessary for the nominal value to be expressed in sterling. They can be shares of one euro each, or one United States dollar each, or one Malaysian ringit each – or whatever currency is thought fit. To avoid ambiguity with units such as dollars, care must be taken to indicate the currency authority – for example, by specifying United States dollars or Commonwealth of Australia dollars. In the case of pounds, sterling will be assumed unless the contrary is indicated.

Subscribers

The subscription clause ('We, the several persons ...') follows clause 5. It does not require a number.

The Memorandum of Association of a private company limited by shares needs to be signed by only one person. For a company limited by guarantee, an unlimited company or a public company, at least two signatures are required.

The persons signing the Memorandum are at this point 'subscribers'. They are not yet shareholders or members since there is not yet a company in which to hold shares. After the documents have been filed at Companies House and a Certificate of Incorporation has been issued, each subscriber automatically becomes a shareholder (or, in the case of a guarantee company, a member) holding the number of shares for which he has subscribed.

A moment's reflection will show that if the Memorandum is signed at the outset by all the persons who will take up shares, there will be no need for a formal allotment of shares (and the filing of a return of allotments) at a later date. However, if the number of intending shareholders is large (more than six or eight, perhaps) or if one or more reside overseas, it may not be practicable for all of them to sign. It may be more convenient for just two or three to sign, the others applying for shares to be allotted at the first board meeting.

Since a company is a 'person', a company can sign the Memorandum. The secretary or a director of the existing company should sign beneath such words as 'for ABC Company Limited', adding 'Secretary' (or 'Director') beneath his or her signature.

Since it is now possible to have a 'single member' company (a company with only one shareholder), it is sufficient if only one person signs the Memorandum of a private company. This is the obvious course if the new company is to be a wholly-owned subsidiary.

Family businesses

Where the purpose of forming the company is to incorporate a partnership or small family business, the choice of subscribers will usually be obvious. A sole trader may sign alone or every partner (even every member of the family) may sign.

The proprietor of a small business may see formal incorporation as an opportunity to pass part of the business to his wife or children without incurring stamp duty or inheritance tax. The value of the shares for which the newcomer subscribes may be within the exemption limits for inheritance tax, and no new tax liability will arise if the company prospers and the shares are later worth many times their value at the time of incorporation. Moreover, profits distributed as dividends to three or four shareholders are likely to attract less income tax than the same sum paid to a single shareholder.

An obvious temptation is for shares to be held 50:50 by husband and wife, but this may carry unforeseen risks. Problems on the death of one partner could be overcome, but what would happen if the marriage were to break down? Neither partner could outvote the other, either could be 'difficult' for reasons that have nothing to do with the company, and the business could be brought to a standstill. These problems could mostly be avoided if the shares are held 51:49 rather than 50:50.

Similarly, the opportunity could be taken to allot shares to a trusted employee – perhaps as a reward for past service or as a strong incentive for the future. Again, however, care is needed. What happens to the shares if the employment is terminated? It may be agreed that the employee retains the shares, but it is not difficult to imagine situations where this would be quite inappropriate. Consideration should be given to preparing a short agreement setting out the circumstances in which the shares should be transferred back. This could be backed up with a blank transfer, as explained below. It is better to deal with such points at the outset than to seek a remedy after an earlier happier relationship has broken down.

If the company is to be registered in Scotland, every subscriber must be aged 16 or over. For companies registered in England (or England and Wales), subscribers need not be of full legal age, but careful thought should be given before allowing anyone below the age of 18 to sign as a subscriber, since the obligation to take up and pay for the shares could not be legally enforced. On reaching age 18 the erstwhile minor could renounce the shares (for instance, if they were not fully paid up) and there could be difficulties if it became necessary to transfer the shares. These problems can be avoided (for example, by appointing a nominee to hold the shares for the minor), but it may be best to seek professional advice, especially if tax-saving is the objective.

Nominee shareholders

Sometimes the person signing the Memorandum is not the beneficial owner – the subscriber is a nominee of the owner. There can be no legal objection to this, but it must be remembered that the company will be entitled to treat the registered holder as the shareholder for all purposes. The nominee will be liable to pay for the shares and will be entitled to vote at general meetings and to receive any dividends or other benefits. However, any problems to which this may give rise can be avoided.

A 'letter of trust' (or 'declaration of trust') should be drawn up and signed (see Draft Wording 10). It is usual to supplement this letter (for practical reasons, not from any legal necessity) with:

(a) A dividend mandate instructing the new company to pay all dividends to the beneficial owner (or to his bank account); and

(b) A 'blank transfer' – a stock transfer form covering the share or shares, signed by the nominee shareholder but leaving blank the date and the name of the person to whom the shares are to be transferred.

This 'blank transfer' is held with the share certificate by the beneficial owner. It does not need to be stamped at the time it is signed. If, later, the parent company wishes to change its nominee – and even if the nominee shareholder is uncooperative – the beneficial owner can complete the blanks, have the transfer form stamped at the fixed rate of £5.00 and present it with the share certificate to have the share(s) transferred to the name of whomever it wishes. Authority to do this is given by the letter of trust.

However, if the nominee were to die, his death would revoke the authority given by the letter of trust. The blank transfer form could not then legally be completed or presented. The beneficial owner would have to ask the executors of the deceased shareholder, on the authority of the letter of trust, to complete a fresh transfer form. This could entail an inconvenient delay while the executors obtain probate and attend to more urgent matters, possibly at a time when the company is facing problems of its own.

In some cases this last problem can be avoided by arranging for shares to be held jointly by two or more persons as joint nominees. Letters of trust and blank transfers are still prepared, but on the death of one of the joint holders all rights and benefits revert to the survivor or survivors under regulation 29 of Table A (or a similar provision in the company's own Articles) and the survivor can then execute such fresh documents as may be required.

The complete draft

At his point it should be possible to prepare an adequate and effective Memorandum comprising the six clauses (five numbered plus the subscription clause) as set out at the start of this chapter. To this should be added the box for signatures. The document should then be circulated to all who may wish to comment. After approval – and amendment if necessary – the names and addresses can be inserted in the signature box, leaving space for a signature above each typed name, and the document is ready for signature.

Form of signature

Each subscriber should sign in ink against the number of shares he will take up. Signature on one copy is sufficient, but it is advisable to keep a second signed copy for the company's own files. Unless (unusually!) each signature is a model of legibility, it would be helpful to print the name beneath each signature. In any case, an individual subscriber's (as distinct from a company subscriber's) occupation and private address should also be shown.

Where one of the subscribers is a company, the secretary or one of the directors of the subscribing (shareholder) company should sign, indicating the capacity in which they are signing – for example,

> Parent Company plc, 100 High Street, London EC2 4YZ, by
> its Secretary,
>
> Peter Smith

Where shares are to be held jointly the names should read:

> John Brown, Engineer, of ....
>
> [PRIVATE ADDRESS]

> jointly with
> David Green, Sales Manager, of ....
>
> [PRIVATE ADDRESS]

and both should sign.

Each signature must be witnessed. It is easiest if both (or all) subscribers sign on the same occasion, when one witness, signing once, will suffice for all. The Articles of Association are signed by the same persons and usually at the same time, but fuller details are given in Chapter 4.

Copies

Although only one copy is essential, it is better to have two signed copies, one for filing with the Registrar of Companies and the other for the company's own files. Later the company will need a dozen or more copies for distribution to bankers, auditors and others. These can readily be prepared by photocopying the company's signed original. In this way it will include the actual signatures of those who signed. If for any reason this is impracticable, the names, addresses, witnesses' names, etc., should be typed into the appropriate spaces before copying.

4 Articles of Association

A private company limited by shares need not register Articles of Association. If it chooses not to do so, Table A – the model set of Articles of Association prescribed by Companies (Tables A to F) Regulations 1985 – will automatically become its Articles of Association. Table A is reproduced as Draft Wording 4. Guarantee companies and unlimited companies must register Articles based, respectively, on Table C and Table E in the Regulations. Subject to this, the following notes on adaptation of the basic Tables will be relevant to all companies.

Many companies find that although most of Table A will suit their requirements, some modification is needed to fit their own special circumstances. A new company therefore has three options:

1 It may register no Articles, in which case Table A in its entirety will operate as the Articles for that company. This course is not recommended.
2 It may register a full set of Articles, replacing – and specifically excluding – the whole of Table A. This may be worthwhile for larger companies, but the extra work and expense are difficult to justify for most of the smaller companies covered by this book.
3 It may register a 'short-form' set of Articles, which modify Table A to the minimum extent necessary for the purposes of that particular company. Table A will then apply to the extent that it is not specifically excluded or overridden by the company's own Articles.

The third course is recommended for the smaller private company limited by shares. It is cheapest, easiest and quickest. Although it can be argued that it is better to have a full set of Articles for a particular company embraced in a single document than a short set, which necessitates reference back to Table A for complete understanding, the inconvenience of referring to two documents can be overcome if Table A (copied from Draft Wording 4 or bought from a legal stationer) is bound together with the company's own Memorandum and Articles, at least for the chairman and secretary. It should not be necessary to supply copies of Table A to the company's bankers, auditors, etc., who may, however, quite properly require copies of the company's own Articles.

In any case, it should be remembered that 'complete understanding' will often require reference also to the Acts, or to other legislation, and to a myriad of legal decisions made under those Acts.

A set of short-form Articles suitable for this type of company is provided in Draft Wording 5.

Short-form Articles – Preamble

The short-form Articles in Draft Wording 5 provide first that Table A shall apply to the company except where specifically excluded or modified; then they list those regulations in Table A which are excluded. After this preamble there follow a number of clauses suitable for smaller private companies. In many cases alternatives are offered, from which selections can be made specifically to suit the company concerned. Drafting to suit a particular company need be no more than making a complete copy of the short-form Articles and deleting whatever is not required.

When all amendments have been made, the Articles must be consecutively numbered. Interpolation of a number – for example, 12A between 12 and 13 – is permitted, but a gap in the numbering is not. It is obviously simplest to renumber throughout.

Classes of shares

Most small companies have only one class of shares, all ranking equally in voting, on dividends and on return of capital if the company should be wound up. In other words, all the shares rank *pari passu* in all respects. Such shares are often referred to as 'ordinary shares', although if there is only the one class they are, strictly speaking, simply 'shares'.

Occasionally the financial structure will require more than one class of shares – commonly 'preference shares' and 'ordinary shares', but possibly designated 'deferred shares', 'non-voting shares', etc. In some circumstances it may be convenient to designate different classes of shares as 'A shares' and 'B shares'. Special rights for separate classes of shares do not need to be set out in the Articles – regulations 2 and 3 of Table A are worded so that such shares can be issued with special rights, those rights being set out in the terms of issue. However, it is clearly convenient to set out the special terms in the Articles so that they can readily be referred to when the need arises, possibly several years later.

The draft short-form Articles provide a selection of alternative wordings, which can be modified as required.

If preference shares are to be issued, it is necessary before drafting to consider:

1 whether they are to be preferred as to dividends or on a return of capital in a winding-up, or both;

2 whether preference dividends are cumulative (i.e., whether any preference dividends unpaid in one year are to be carried forward to take priority in later years) and, if so, whether the arrears are to carry interest;

3 whether the preference shares should participate in dividends beyond the preferential rate (for example, they may carry a five per cent preferential dividend, but whenever a dividend of more than five per cent is paid on the ordinary shares, the preference shares may be entitled to that same higher rate);

4 whether holders may vote at shareholders' meetings:
   - always; or
   - never; or
   - only if preference dividends are in arrear; or
   - only if preference shareholders' rights are directly affected; or
   - only in other specified circumstances.

Various combinations of these alternatives are of course possible. Usually preference shares are preferential as to dividends and on a return of capital, and holders may vote:

> ... only if preference dividends are unpaid for six months or more or if any of the special rights and privileges of preference shareholders would be directly affected by the matter upon which the vote is to be taken.

Future increases in share capital

If, after the company is formed, it is decided to increase the share capital, this can readily be done and the procedure is set out in Chapter 12. Power to increase the share capital must be included in the Articles, but this is covered by regulation 32 of Table A. The directors must also be authorised to allot the new shares, either by the Articles or by a resolution of the shareholders in general meeting. This is not covered by Table A so, unless the shareholders see some special need to keep the matter under their own control, the necessary authority should be given by the Articles – even though that power will only be valid for five years. Clause 7 in the short-form Articles covers this point.

New shares must first be offered to shareholders in proportion to their existing holdings unless some other arrangement is sanctioned by a special resolution of the shareholders, but a private company can opt out of this by a suitable regulation in its Articles. This point is covered by clause 8 in the short-form Articles.

CHAPTER 4

Common seal

Until 1989 it was usual for even the smallest company to have a common seal, a cumbersome embossing device for executing certain documents. Since this is no longer necessary, it will be assumed throughout this book that a newly formed company will not have a common seal. It will therefore be advisable to delete all references to the common seal throughout Table A. Suitable wording is included in the short-form Articles (clause 9).

Partly paid shares

It is unusual nowadays for companies to issue partly paid shares. Regulations 8–22 and 57 of Table A have relevance only if there are partly paid shares. Where a full set of Articles will be registered, therefore, its length can be considerably reduced by omitting all those regulations and substituting briefly:

> **15** The company shall not issue shares otherwise than fully paid on allotment.

Where only a short set of Articles will be registered, the regulations in question will cause no inconvenience.

Share pre-emption

For some companies, particularly the smaller family business, the question of share pre-emption – the right of existing shareholders to buy out or have first refusal over the shares of other shareholders – can be a matter of great importance, and so a separate chapter (Chapter 5) has been devoted to this subject. The recommendation there is that such arrangements are better set out in a shareholders' agreement than in the Articles, but if for some good reason they are included in the Articles they should be inserted after regulation 35 of Table A, or in the equivalent position if a full set of Articles is to be registered.

Shareholders' votes

Regulations 36–53 of Table A relate to general meetings (known also as members' meetings or shareholders' meetings). They largely repeat requirements of the Act, and in most cases it is not only undesirable but impossible to alter them. Much the same may be said of regulations 55–63 (voting, polls and proxies).

Regulation 54 of Table A requires special thought. It provides that on a show of hands every member shall have one vote and on a poll every member shall have one vote for each share held. This seems fair enough for a large company with hundreds or thousands of shareholders; but what if there are only two, of whom one holds 30 per cent and the other 70 per cent of the shares? Is it intended that the larger shareholder shall always be able to demand a poll and outvote the smaller shareholder? Alternatively, in the case of a special resolution (requiring a 75 per cent majority), is it intended that the minority holder should always be able to frustrate the wishes of the larger shareholder? Both are possible and may be desirable in some circumstances but lead to deadlock in others. This is clearly an area where discussion must be initiated and careful instructions taken. A little thought before incorporation may save much time and frustration later.

A useful device is to designate shares as 'A shares' (all of which are held by one shareholder) and 'B shares' (all held by the other). In most situations each share will carry one vote, but in special circumstances specified by the Articles every A share may carry one vote while every B share carries, say, five votes.

A similar device can ensure fair representation on the board of directors. The provisions in Table A for directors to be appointed by voting in general meeting can be replaced by a regulation on the lines:

> The holder or holders of all the A shares shall collectively be entitled to appoint three directors and may remove any director they have appointed. If the number of directors appointed by the holder or holders of the A shares shall at any time fall below three then they may appoint an additional director to fill that vacancy.

> The holder or holders of all the B shares shall collectively be entitled to appoint two directors and may remove any director they have appointed. If the number of directors appointed by the holder or holders of the B shares shall at any time fall below two then they may appoint an additional director to fill that vacancy.

After establishing the desired procedure, any voting restraints may be incorporated either in the Articles or in a separate shareholders' agreement. Use of the Articles is usually thought practicable only if the provisions are relatively simple. Examples are given in alternative clauses 11 of the short-form Articles. Where they are complex, and particularly if they are for any reason confidential, it is probably better to include a suitable clause in the shareholders' agreement. Legal advice may then be necessary.

CHAPTER 4

Directors and board meetings

For many small companies, regulations 64, 70–72 and 81–98 of Table A are likely to prove acceptable. However, where special arrangements are to apply to the number or the manner of appointment of directors, this is the point at which to insert the special requirements. Alternative wordings are given in clauses 13 of the short-form Articles.

Regulations 65–69 of Table A (alternate directors) may seem unnecessary for many small family businesses, but they can enable a company to surmount an unexpected problem such as the long illness of a director, so it is recommended they be included even if they are unlikely ever to be used.

However, regulations 73–75 and 80 (retirement of directors in rotation) will prove meaningless and irritating for many small companies, in which case they should be excluded. Care should be taken not to exclude regulation 79, which empowers the board to co-opt an additional director.

Borrowing powers

Table A of earlier Companies Acts restricted the borrowing powers of directors. The current Table A does not limit directors' borrowing powers in any way. Whether this is appropriate for the particular company about to be formed needs to be considered carefully. Where share ownership and management control are closely linked, as in a small family business or in a group of companies with close financial control, it is probably unnecessary to limit borrowing by means of the Articles. But in other cases the unrestricted power to run up a large overdraft or to borrow money in other ways may be a formula for disaster. To guard against this, the directors' borrowing powers can be limited either to a stated maximum sum or by a formula related, for instance, to issued share capital or to issued capital plus reserves. Suitable wordings will be found in the short-form Articles.

In every case the draft regulations have been so worded that the borrowing limit can be increased by the shareholders at any time, thus minimising the formality if the limit is found to be too restrictive. In this way control is left in the hands of the shareholders.

Special articles

After preparation of the short-form Articles, it would be prudent to read Table A to consider whether any further changes are desirable. These should be made only after due consideration and for good reason, lest they introduce an undesirable element of uncertainty. Change of wording for the sake of being different, though not unknown, is not recommended.

Signature of Articles

The Articles of Association must be signed by the same persons and in the same manner as the Memorandum of Association, except that the number of shares to be taken does not appear against each name. It will clearly be convenient to sign both documents at the same time. As with the Memorandum, it is advisable to have two copies signed, one for filing with the Registrar of Companies and the other for the company's own files.

Copies

It is usual to have the Memorandum of Association bound together with the Articles of Association as if they were a single document. At a later stage, more copies will be required for distribution to directors, bankers, auditors and others, and these can readily be prepared by photocopying the originals so that they include the signatures of those who signed. If for any reason this is impracticable, the names, addresses, witnesses' names, etc., should be typed into the appropriate spaces before copying.

A small stock of spare copies may be useful. Any shareholder is entitled to ask for a copy. Although a small charge can be made, this is rarely demanded.

5 Shareholders' Agreements

If there will be more than one shareholder, consideration should be given to whether, in addition to the 'Companies Act' documents required to form the company, an agreement between the shareholders (or at least between the principal shareholders) would be useful. Such an agreement might include:

1 a statement of the business relationship between the parties;
2 an agreement on objectives (budgets or expansion plans could be included, possibly as schedules);
3 a commitment to provide further funds as the business expands, whether by increasing the share capital, by giving personal guarantees for bank loans, or in other ways;
4 for some shareholders, a limitation on the liability to provide further funds (otherwise a dominant, possibly wealthy, shareholder may try after a few years to increase his participation in a successful company at the expense of other shareholders unable to match the dominant party's ambitions);
5 an agreement that in certain circumstances, such as failure to reach output targets, the business is to be discontinued and the company wound up;
6 pre-emption terms to establish rules and calculate a fair price if a shareholder wishes to sell shares – either to raise money or to bring in a new shareholder – or on death or insolvency;
7 the action to be taken if a corporate shareholder is itself taken over;
8 in the case of a company formed to run a professional practice, the action to be taken if one director and/or one shareholder loses his professional qualification.

Clearly some of these items could also find their way into the Articles of Association of the company, in which event it will be most important to ensure that the two documents are consistent. Some items would be quite inappropriate in the Articles of Association. For example, it is all very well for one shareholder to undertake to guarantee the bank overdraft if circumstances require, but if such a promise appeared in the Articles and were therefore public knowledge, bargaining with the bank manager might prove difficult.

In a choice whether to include certain provisions in the Articles or in a shareholders' agreement, it must be admitted that nearly all the advantages lie in a separate shareholders' agreement that remains confidential. Yet there is apt to be difficulty: some intending shareholders, having seen such provisions in the Articles of other companies, may expect or even insist on their inclusion in the Articles. However, there are strong arguments against this. Provisions of the kind we have mentioned do not usually concern the Registrar of Companies, the company's creditors, the journalists who scan the files of each new company at Companies House or the bank manager, who will inevitably ask for a copy of the Articles. Indeed, there may quite properly be confidential arrangements between the larger shareholders that are of no concern to the minority. A shareholders' agreement preserves that confidentiality, whereas the Articles are on public record, open to inspection by anyone in return for a modest fee.

The second, arguably stronger, reason for preferring to put such clauses in a shareholders' agreement rather than the Articles is that, if circumstances or attitudes change, fresh agreement can be reached and recorded quietly and quickly. The formality, publicity and risk of failure associated with a special resolution to change the Articles are avoided, as is the risk that the inevitable publicity may prejudice negotiations with third parties.

If the terms to be agreed are simple, an exchange of letters may suffice. If they are more complex, legal advice beyond the scope of this book may be necessary. However, careful thought given to what is written above should save time and expense, as well as ensuring that essential aspects are not overlooked.

Pre-emption agreements

A pre-emption agreement – or a pre-emption clause in a more general shareholders' agreement – is one that gives one party the right in specified circumstances to buy out the shares of another party or to have 'first refusal' if another wishes to sell. Care is needed in defining the circumstances, but it is also important to establish a procedure to determine a fair price for shares for which there is and can be no open market.

Three types of company

This book is primarily concerned with three types of company. One is the wholly-owned subsidiary, in which there can be no possibility of conflict between shareholders. If this is the type of company with which you are concerned, you may safely skip the rest of this chapter.

The second type of company is the joint venture, established to provide a legal framework to the relationship between business partners (individuals or companies) who have no basis for cooperation beyond that comprised in the documents which establish the company. Questions that need to be considered are: What will happen to the shareholdings if the business fails, if the parties disagree beyond the possibility of reconciliation or if one party, for whatever reason, wishes to sell his shares?

Then there is the family company. It might be thought that there is little risk of conflict here; but the possibility of a broken marriage or family disagreement cannot be ruled out. However harmonious family relationships may appear at the outset, it would be wise – indeed, it could be the duty of a professional adviser – to consider how the company and its shareholders would resolve their problems in the event of family disagreement. Most of what follows in relation to a joint-venture company is therefore relevant to a family business.

Possible difficulties

The obvious difficulties are that the problems are hypothetical. At a time when everyone is ready and willing to agree, we are trying to envisage circumstances of fundamental disagreement and we are trying to determine, long before the event, how such fundamental disagreements can be resolved fairly. If – in these hypothetical circumstances – shares have to be transferred, a price must be paid for them, and we may have to lay down a formula for valuation at a time when we cannot know whether the business will be a success or a failure or whether, for example, the fairest way of assessing the worth of the shares would be a 'net assets' basis, an 'earnings' basis, dividend yield or something quite different. And the professional adviser may have to present these problems to the parties for their agreement at a time when the possibility of dissolution of the partnership is furthest from their thoughts.

Enquiries on pre-emption clauses are frequently answered with: 'Include the standard clause'. There is no such thing. At best there will be a series of alternative 'standard' clauses – one for the husband-and-wife company, one for the extended family, one for the joint venture between equal partners and (most difficult of all) one for the unequal partnership between an individual entrepreneur/manager and a powerful company that is providing finance and other resources.

Similarly, it is often assumed that all questions of share valuation can be 'left to the auditors'. In the past that was perhaps true; accounting methods and hence the ways of valuing shares were once less varied and less open to dispute than they are today. But in recent years we have seen legal action brought on the grounds that shares have been valued on the wrong basis, and auditors are now, with justification, much more cautious. Clearly, therefore, this is a subject that should be discussed with the intended auditors before drafting. First, are they willing to undertake a valuation in some unknown (and unknowable) future circumstances? Second, what instructions would they expect to receive in that event? It is most unlikely that they will be willing to act on instructions simply to 'value the shares'; at the very least, some indication of the basis of valuation will be indispensable.

Finally, it should be noted that we need to deal only with the situation where there is disagreement. If there are a willing seller and a willing buyer, if they are able to agree a price and if neither the board of directors nor any other shareholder objects, then there is no reason why the parties should not go ahead on their own terms, ignoring any pre-existing agreement. Only if objections are raised will the terms of a pre-emption clause be brought into play, and even then they will usually serve as a starting-point for discussion rather than as an inflexible basis for valuation.

Trigger points

How, then, do we proceed? We must first consider the circumstances that might lead to a transfer of shares. For example:

1 A shareholder may die. Will the remaining shareholders be content to find themselves in partnership with a surviving spouse or other legatee, or would they wish to buy the shares from the executors?
2 In the foregoing case, would they wish merely to have the right to buy, or would they also give the executors the right to require them to buy?
3 A shareholder may become bankrupt. Similar questions arise.
4 A corporate shareholder may be taken over by a business competitor.
5 A corporate shareholder may go into liquidation, or a receiver may be appointed.
6 A shareholder may compete with the company, take employment with a competitor or acquire a company (or an interest in a company) that competes.
7 A shareholder may commit some breach of the shareholders' agreement.
8 Where the company is established to run a professional practice and

one of the shareholders loses his or her professional qualification, it may be essential that the others buy that shareholder out if the practice is to continue within the relevant professional code.

9 Where a small shareholding is issued to a manager, the manager's contract of employment may be terminated. Will that manager then be entitled to retain the shares or be required to sell them back to the majority shareholders?

10 What if expansion of the business requires additional capital and some of the shareholders are unable or unwilling to contribute their proportion?

These are the circumstances most likely to trigger a pre-emption clause, but there may well be others in special cases.

Notice

Having set out the circumstances by which, for the particular company, the pre-emption clause is to be triggered, we must give consideration to the way in which pre-emption rights are to be brought into operation, for example:

1 Which party is entitled to take the initiative?
2 To whom does the party give notice?
3 If (as usually) notice is given to the company secretary, whom does the secretary notify?
4 What time limits, if any, apply between each stage – e.g.,
 • the event that triggers pre-emption (e.g. death of a shareholder);
 • notice by the intending purchaser to the company secretary;
 • notice by the secretary to the other shareholders (or some of them);
 • a request to the auditors to value;
 • notice of the value to intended buyer(s) and seller(s);
 • acceptance of valuation;
 • exchange of money against title.

Valuation

The point has already been made that the method of valuation must be acceptable to the person who has to make that valuation, and he may ask a number of questions before making a proposal – for example:

1 Which of the usual accounting methods (net assets, earnings, dividend yield, etc.) is to be used? With some companies one basis – say,

net assets – may be appropriate in the early years, but earnings may be a more relevant measure once the company is established. In any case, a pre-emption clause is virtually useless and only likely to lead to dispute if this point is not settled long before the clause is invoked.

2 Is the valuation to be based on the last audited accounts, the next audited accounts (which would straddle the event which triggered pre-emption but could cause delay) or mid-year accounts drawn up (at extra expense) especially for the purpose?

3 What adjustments, if any, are to be made to the audited accounts for pre-emption valuation – e.g. for profits earned or other changes in net current assets since the balance sheet date, or for changes in issued capital? This can usually be covered by wording such as:

> ... after making such adjustments as they think fair and equitable having regard to profits earned, losses realised, or changes in value of assets or liabilities since the date of the last audited balance sheet preceding the date of the valuation.

4 Who pays for the valuation – and any extra accounting work entailed?

5 When or by what instalments is the price to be paid? Not infrequently there will be a 'retention'. For example, there may be a payment of 80 per cent of the agreed price on signing the documents, leaving the remaining 20 per cent to be paid on completion of the next audit. At that time adjustments can be made for facts not known at the time of transfer of the shares or for a proportion of the year's profits attributable to the period prior to the transfer.

Conclusion

Pre-emption terms are, for reasons of confidentiality and convenience, better in a shareholders' agreement than in the Articles. When careful thought has been given to the points raised in this chapter, suitable instructions should be given to the solicitor responsible for preparing that agreement. But be warned that intentions stated at a time when all agree may not be a reliable guide to performance after disagreement.

6 Directors' Interests

The law relating to directors' interests in contracts is widely mis-understood and often ignored. The penalty for non-compliance is a fine of £1,000 or more, but more serious consequences can follow. Some of these can be avoided by including suitable wording in the Articles of Association, but consideration must be given to the propriety of 'contracting out' in this way. A watchful eye must always be kept at board meetings so that directors may protect themselves by disclosing any interest they may have in a contract under discussion.

When it has been decided what should and what should not be permitted, suitable wording should be incorporated in the Articles. There are three points to be considered: first, whether directors should be permitted to make contracts with the company at all; second, if they do so, whether they must 'declare their interest' in the contract at a board meeting; and finally, whether such a director can vote at a board meeting on the question of whether the company should enter into the contract.

What is an interest in a contract?

In law, 'contract' means 'agreement'. Thus a director of a trading company who agrees to buy from or sell to that company is making contracts with the company. If by so doing he secures some financial advantage, he has an interest in the contract.

Apart from the obvious case, where a director buys from or sells to the company, we must consider indirect interests. For example, a person may be a director (or a shareholder, or both) in two companies. If those companies enter into a contract the director will be *indirectly* interested on both sides and will have to disclose his or her interest at board meetings of both companies. If he fails to do so, the contract may be unenforceable. He may even have to pay over to the company (or, worse, to both companies!) any gain he or his associates make from the contract.

In all such cases, directors must disclose their interest in a contract to their fellow directors. There is no way of avoiding this. Subject to that, it is possible to avoid most of the adverse consequences by including suitable wording in the company's Articles of Association.

The law

A director occupies a position of trust. If directors make a personal profit (whether at the company's expense or at the expense of someone else) when acting for the company, the position at common law is that they must pay over the profit to the company. Moreover, they cannot enforce the contract against the company.

However, this very strict rule of law can be modified by a company's Articles, which may permit a director to enter into such a contract and even to retain any resulting profit. Regulation 85 of Table A (Draft Wording 4) does this, as explained below.

Articles often provide that directors shall not vote at a board meeting and shall not be counted in the quorum on any contract in which they have an interest. However, this could sometimes make it impossible for small companies to muster a quorum of 'disinterested' directors. Regulation 94 of Table A sets out the circumstances in which a director may or may not vote.

Declaring an interest

Section 317(1) of the Act requires that a director who has any interest in a contract made with a company must 'declare his interest' at a board meeting. The Articles cannot waive this duty. Section 317(2) sets out rules as to the time when the declaration should be made but can be summed up by the words 'as early as possible'. Sections 330 and 346 extend the requirement so that in the case of loans and similar transactions the director must declare an interest if a 'connected person' (for example, a spouse, a child under the age of 18 or a business partner) has an interest in a contract.

Section 317(3), however, permits directors to give general notice in advance that are interested in all contracts that may be made in future with named companies or partnerships of which they are a member (but if their interest is that of a director or creditor, specific disclosure is required on every occasion).

Thus it has become usual for directors at the first board meeting of a newly formed company to present a list of companies in which they are shareholders and therefore deemed 'interested'. Obviously, to provide evidence to protect the director, the disclosure should be recorded in the minutes of the meeting. Suitable wording will be found in the draft minutes for the first board meeting (Draft Wording 7).

CHAPTER 6

This type of general disclosure is particularly suitable for joint-venture companies that have been set up for the very purpose of contracting with their shareholder companies. It is also suitable for groups of companies where shareholdings and directorships often overlap.

Such a general declaration of interests does not, however, absolve the secretary and each director from reviewing the position whenever a new contract is considered at a board meeting.

Articles of Association

Articles of Association invariably soften the harsh implications of the legal position, but the extent to which they do so depends on the purpose of the company and the relationship between the shareholders. Taking Table A as our starting-point, regulations 85 and 94–98 provide a sound basis for most small companies (including family businesses, subsidiaries and joint ventures), and it is recommended that changes be made only for good reason. Points for consideration are:

1 Are shareholders adequately protected from selfish directors?
2 Is there a danger that the proceedings of the board will frequently be brought to a standstill because there are not enough 'disinterested' directors to form a quorum? (The occasional *impasse* can be overcome by holding a shareholders' meeting as explained below.)
3 Is there some situation peculiar to the company under consideration, as might exist with a subsidiary in a large group of companies that frequently makes contracts with other members of the group?

Table A

The obligation to disclose interests in contracts comes from the Companies Acts, not from Table A, but regulation 85 of Table A provides that if a director has declared an interest he, or any company or partnership in which he has a stake, may freely contract with the company and the director will not have to hand over any resultant profits.

Regulation 94, however, provides that, even if he has declared an interest, a director may not vote on a contract in which he has a financial interest. There are certain exceptions listed in Table A. Regulation 95 states that a director who cannot vote may not be counted in the quorum. As a consequence, it may be impossible for the board to reach a decision because it cannot form a 'disinterested' quorum. However, Table A permits the restrictions on voting to be suspended wholly or in part by the shareholders in general meeting.

This should meet most requirements. If a director is proposing to enter into a contract directly with the company of which he is a director, it is probably in the best interests of the company either that he should leave the voting to a quorum of directors who are not 'interested' or, if that is not possible, that the situation should come to the notice of the shareholders.

Ratification by a meeting of shareholders

The rules concerning interests in contracts apply to directors, not to shareholders – who are not in a position of trust and are expected to act in their own interests. Hence there are no restrictions on voting by shareholders at general meetings.

It is sometimes argued that a new company's own Articles should delete or substantially modify regulations 94 and 95 (for example in a family business where all shareholders are also directors and may often find themselves dealing with the company). However, this is not necessary. If the board of directors cannot reach a decision because most or all of the directors are precluded from voting, the board can simply convene a shareholders' meeting to be held immediately. If all the shareholders are present (or, if the shareholder is a company, represented) the usual 14 or 21 days' notice can be waived. The director who was precluded from voting as a director is now free to vote as a shareholder. The contract can be approved, the shareholders' meeting closed and the board meeting resumed.

If, however, one or more shareholders are not present at the board meeting, it will be necessary to hold the shareholders' meeting later so that the absentee(s) may be given the usual period of notice. Arguably this is only fair anyway!

Board minutes

Suitable wording for board minutes will be found in Draft Wording 7.

It must be remembered that there is an on-going obligation for all directors to disclose their interests as they arise or as new contracts are entered into. Draft Wording 7 can readily be adapted to meet any likely circumstances.

7 Accounting Reference Date

The accounting reference date is the date of the annual balance sheet, the date to which the annual accounts are made up. The accounting period (the period covered by the trading and profit and loss accounts) is the interval been two successive accounting reference dates. Unless other arrangements are made, the accounting reference date will automatically become the last day of the month in which the company is incorporated, and the first accounting reference period will be one year, or a few days longer to the end of the month.

If this date does not suit the company, it can be changed by sending Form 225 to Companies House (Form 224 is now obsolete), but the new date must not shorten the first accounting reference period to less than six months or lengthen it to more than 18 months. Form 225 may be filed at the outset, with the other papers required to register a new company, or at a later date after the board of directors has given the matter due thought.

The accounting reference date must be a particular date in the year – for example, 30 June and not 'the last Saturday in June'. However, section 227(2) of the Act permits accounts to be made up either to the accounting reference date or to such other date, not more than seven days before or after the accounting reference date, as the directors may decide. Thus if the accounting reference date as filed is, say, 28 June, the accounts could always be made up to the last Saturday in June, irrespective of the date on which that day falls. This flexibility could suit some accounting systems or could allow stocktaking always to take place over a weekend.

The accounting reference date of a subsidiary must normally coincide with that of the parent company, unless in the opinion of the parent company directors there are good reasons against it. (Apart from business convenience, a desire to minimise or defer tax can be a 'good reason', but one should be circumspect in stating this by way of explanation.) Note that it is the opinion of the parent company directors which is relevant – the assumption seems to be that the directors of a wholly-owned subsidiary just do as they are told!

Choice of date

Where business, profits and cash all flow evenly throughout the year, the choice of date may not be a matter of great moment. A date approximately one year after incorporation may be convenient, or a later date may be preferred so as to defer for as long as possible the work of preparing and auditing the first set of accounts.

Tax may be a relevant consideration and should be discussed with the company's accountants, auditors or other tax advisers. The choice of date will not affect the amount of tax payable but could significantly affect the date on which it is due and hence the period for which cash remains in the business as working capital.

From the standpoint of business convenience, time can most readily be spared for preparing accounts when other work is slack and not too many of the accounts staff are on annual leave. In most businesses the pressure of work in preparing the annual accounts will start about four or six weeks after the accounting reference date – to allow for late receipt of invoices, remittances, etc. – and continue for two or three months after that. According to the nature of the company's business, there may be other considerations – for example, stocktaking may be easiest when stock is at its lowest.

Thus the ideal accounting reference date may be:

1 the day in the year when stock is lowest (to simplify stocktaking);
2 one to three months before the slackest time of the year (to level out pressure on staff);
3 as long as possible after the busiest, most profitable time of the year, (so that tax on the profits remains in the business as long as possible).

It may be difficult to reconcile these requirements!

Corporation tax

It is beyond the scope of this book to cover taxation in any detail. Specialist advice may be necessary. The objective here is to draw attention to those aspects of corporation tax that may influence the choice of accounting reference date.

Corporation tax is assessed by reference to the year ending 31 March. If the company's accounting reference date is 31 March, corporation tax will be based on profits for the accounting reference period. If some other date is chosen for the accounting reference date, taxable profits will be ascertained by apportioning profits from two accounting years.

If profits are expected to flow evenly throughout the year, the choice of accounting reference date will not matter greatly. But if the business is highly seasonal, or if profits are expected to increase sharply year after year, a judicious choice of accounting reference date may have a beneficial effect on cash flow. It could be well worth while estimating income, expenses, profits and cash flow month by month for the first 18 or 24 months and spending an hour at a computer screen with a spreadsheet to see whether one accounting reference date rather than another produces a significant change. But deferral of tax should not be the only or even the main objective. Against any saving in overdraft interest must be set the inconvenience and cost of extra work. It is better to make more profits and pay more tax than to incur more expense and end up with lower profits!

8 Filing the Documents

When all the necessary documents have been prepared, they should be collated, signed and filed with the Registrar of Companies (see Directory).

Documents to be filed

The documents to be filed comprise:

- the Memorandum of Association;
- the Articles of Association (usually stapled with the Memorandum as a single document);
- Form 10 (first directors, secretary and registered office) with Form 10 (continuation) if there are to be joint secretaries or more than two directors (or pages 2 and 3 of Form 10 itself if Form 10 (continuation) is not available;
- Form 12 (declaration of compliance);
- Form 225 (accounting reference date). This form may be filed later – up to 12 months after incorporation (see Chapter 7).
- if any document is in Welsh, an English translation certified by a solicitor or notary public.
- the £20 registration fee.

The registration fee is usually paid by credit card to eliminate any possible delay. If payment is made by cheque, it must be payable to 'Companies House' and crossed 'A/c payee'.

No covering letter is required unless some point requires explanation (for example, if a request is made for the company to be incorporated on a particular date or if application is made for the use of one of the 'specified' words in the company name).

Form of documents – printing

The Act empowers the Registrar of Companies to prescribe requirements for the paper (size, weight, quality and colour) and printing (size, typeface, colour, etc.) of documents for registration. In practice, however, documents will be accepted if they are:

- standard A4 size;
- durable;
- in black type on white paper;
- easily legible.

No problems will arise with the preprinted forms obtained from Companies House. If you print your own, you should ensure that they are of acceptable quality and clarity. Take particular care with the Memorandum and Articles of Association, which will necessarily be prepared in house.

The requirement for legibility will be met by printing with an ink-jet or a laser printer, using a standard typeface. Documents produced on a dot-matrix printer are unlikely to be accepted. Good-quality photocopies are acceptable, but you should examine any photocopies carefully to check that they are of sufficient quality. Signatures (which should not, of course, be photocopies on the documents for filing) may be ink or ball-point and should preferably be in black (even though blue is acceptable).

Signatures

Before filing, check that all the forms have been correctly signed. It may be convenient to hold a short meeting at which the documents can be passed round for signature – except Form 12, which is more conveniently signed later. Signatures are required as follows:

1 The subscriber or subscribers (first shareholders) must sign:
   - the Memorandum;
   - the Articles;
   - Form 10.
2 A witness (possibly more than one, according to circumstances) must also sign the Memorandum and Articles. The company secretary could sign as witness.
3 Each of the intended directors must sign Form 10 or, if there are more than two directors, Form 10 (continuation). If one of the directors is unable to sign at the outset, it may save time to omit his name from Form 10, wait until the company is formed and then appoint him as an additional director at the first board meeting. He will then have to sign Form 288a, which must be filed within 14 days of that board meeting (see Chapter 12).

4 The intended secretary must sign:
- Form 10;
- Form 225 (if it is filed at this stage);
- Form 12. This form must be signed in the presence of a Justice of the Peace or a Commissioner for Oaths. (Most Commissioners are also solicitors. If you do not know one, look in Y
person may also sign the Memorandum and Articles as witness to the subscribers' signatures.

5 The JP or Commissioner will also sign Form 12 (and will charge a fee, usually about £5.00).

6 The cheque or credit card voucher must be signed in the usual way. (Note that the company itself, not yet being incorporated, will not at this point have a bank account of its own.)

Dating the forms

Every signature must be dated. For simplicity, the same date should be used throughout, but no date must be later than that on Form 12.

Filing

When the forms have been completed and signed, make copies for the company's own files and take or send the originals to the Registrar of Companies in an envelope clearly marked: 'NEW COMPANY'. Although not essential, it is a good idea to request acknowledgment of the documents and to enclose a stamped addressed envelope. Companies House will not send a receipt unless specifically asked.

The address for companies whose registered office will be in England or Wales is: Companies House, Crown Way, Cardiff, CF14 3UZ. But documents intended for Cardiff can also be delivered to any of the offices of the Registrar of Companies listed in the Directory. For companies whose registered office is to be in Scotland the documents should be taken or sent to: Companies House, 37 Castle Terrace, Edinburgh, EH1 2EB.

The Registrar aims to issue Certificates of Incorporation within five working days, but you should allow longer if possible in case of postal or other delays. If there is some special urgency, arrangements can be made for same-day incorporation, but the standard £20 fee then becomes £100 and the envelope should be marked: 'NEW COMPANY – SAME DAY'.

If any error has been made, the Registrar will return the erroneous form, which should be corrected. The alteration should be signed (not just initialled) by the person(s) who signed the original form. If all is well, however – and it should be if these instructions have been followed – the Registrar will issue the Certificate of Incorporation and the company will be incorporated from the date typed on that certificate.

The certificate will be sent by post to the person named on Form 10 as filing the documents. This is usually the secretary-designate of the new company, but it could be, for example, the parent company. The company about to be incorporated must not be named as filing the documents, since it is not yet in existence when they are sent for filing.

9 First Board Meeting

Why and when?

The company exists from the moment the Registrar of Companies issues the Certificate of Incorporation, but until it has held its first board meeting many routine items of business (such as drawing cheques) may prove difficult or impossible. This meeting cannot be held until the date shown on the Certificate of Incorporation, but it should be held as soon as possible thereafter.

A draft notice and agenda paper, combined in a single document, is shown in Draft Wording 6, and draft minutes for the same meeting appear as Draft Wording 7. These will be largely self-explanatory, but the following notes may help to deal with unusual circumstances.

Preliminary points

A copy of the notice and agenda (adapted to the needs of the particular company), should be sent to every director, including any whom the company intends to appoint at the meeting.

Although it is necessary to give every director formal notice of a meeting, it is arguable that, as a matter of strict law, it is not necessary to send them an agenda paper. Directors (unlike shareholders) have a duty to attend meetings, whatever items of business may or may not be intended. However, it is sound business practice to send out as full an agenda paper as possible so that directors can give preliminary thought to the matters to be discussed.

Often the notice of the meeting appears on a separate sheet from the agenda. The convenience and economy of combining them (as in Draft Wording 6) will be obvious.

There is a strict, logical sequence for the items. The meeting cannot proceed to business until you have established that you have a company, that the meeting is properly constituted and that the proper directors are present. You cannot do anything else until you have appointed a chairman. A company secretary is essential to ensure, *inter alia*, that every decision is recorded in the minutes and subsequently implemented. You are strongly recommended not to vary the order of the items. Other business can of course be added at the end.

Appointment of directors and other officers

The first directors and the secretary will have been appointed by Form 10 (now filed at Companies House), and nothing further is required to establish them in office. However, since it is desirable, even if not strictly necessary, that the minute book should record all such appointments, the names of the first officers are included in the minutes of the first board meeting.

Where only some of the directors were appointed by Form 10, additional directors can now be appointed by a board resolution, and suitable wording is given. Each new director will have to sign their consent to act on Form 288a, and it will be convenient to have the form(s) available for signature at the meeting (or signed beforehand). The company secretary must also sign these before filing them at Companies House.

Similarly, it is desirable (if not strictly necessary) to report and record in the minutes the full address of the registered office and (if it has been fixed at this stage) the accounting reference date.

Bank account

The bank with which an account is to be opened should be determined prior to the meeting and its printed form for opening a company account should be obtained, preferably in duplicate. This form comprises three parts:

1 A request to the bank to open the account, stating that copies of the Memorandum and Articles of Association and the (original) Certificate of Incorporation are enclosed. The certificate will of course be returned after examination. Some printed bank forms also request the certificate to commence business, but that is appropriate only for a public company. For a private company any such reference should be deleted.
2 A 'certified resolution'. This is an extract from the minutes covering the opening of the bank account, setting out the way it is to be operated, who is to sign cheques and any other special instructions. The resolution must be certified as a correct copy by an officer of the company. In other circumstances the signature of either the chairman or the secretary would be sufficient, but in this case, since the resolution will almost certainly authorise both of these to sign

cheques, the bank will require at least two signatures to the certified resolution.

The resolution as printed in the bank's printed form is certified to be a true extract from the minute book. In practice, it works the other way around. The bank's form is completed and signed, and the relevant part is then copied into the minutes. You should not overlook the need to make a copy of the form before returning it to the bank in order complete the minute book.

3 A list of the persons authorised to sign, with a specimen signature of each. The office held by each signatory (chairman, director, secretary, etc.) is usually also stated.

The resolution set out in the bank's printed form is usually quite suitable for the average small company, but it should not be adopted without thought. Banks will usually accept reasonable amendments to their printed wording. Careful thought should be given to signatures. Apart from considering the obvious possibilities for internal fraud, you should ensure that signing arrangements safeguard the company against external fraud (for example, the inadvertent payment of amounts for which the company is not really liable). A useful checklist follows:

1 Every cheque (or every cheque above a stated value) should be signed by at least two persons.

2 To minimise the risk of collusion, avoid a 'manager and assistant' combination – i.e., a situation where one employee or one director may sign a cheque and then insist that his assistant also sign. With a large staff this can be ensured by wording the resolution: '... if signed by any one person from Panel A below and countersigned by any one person from Panel B'. Panel A could comprise senior staff from the administrative departments while Panel B could comprise seniors from the commercial departments. The managing director could be named in both panels, but, to avoid misunderstanding, the resolution could include: '... but no person shall sign in a dual capacity'.)

3 Do not give signing authority to those responsible for the cash book or ledgers.

4 Try to arrange that, even if one signature is that of a busy person who could on occasion sign without proper thought, the other will always be that of someone who will take enough time to consider whether the payment ought to be made at all.

5 At the same time, regard must be paid to business convenience. It would be unwise to be so restrictive that at times of holidays, illness or other crisis there is delay or difficulty in getting cheques signed at all. This may present serious problems in a small office, so it is some-

times arranged that year-round authority is given to a very restricted number of persons. If one of those is unavoidably absent for more than a few days a special board meeting can pass an additional resolution:

> That _____ Bank plc be authorised to pay cheques drawn on behalf of the company if signed between 23 July and 14 August 2000, both days inclusive, by Ms _____ in place of Mr _____.'

A specimen signature of the new signatory must be supplied to the bank, and it will be convenient to provide this at the foot of the sheet of paper bearing the certified copy of the board's resolution.

Once it has been resolved who is to sign, the bank's printed form may be completed and taken to the board meeting so that the directors and other officers can provide their specimen signatures as soon as the resolution has been passed. If signatures are required of persons not attending the meeting (such as managers who are not directors) these can readily be obtained later (or even before the meeting), but if any signature cannot be supplied owing to illness or absence abroad the form should be returned to the bank with signatures missing. They can follow later on a sheet of blank paper on which has been typed:

XYZ Limited

Specimen Signature

Mr John Smith, a director, will sign . . . .

Share certificates

Share certificates should be prepared beforehand so that they can be signed at the meeting. Law stationers sell suitable forms (usually in books of 12 or more) with a blank space where the name of the company can be typed above the printed word 'Limited'. There is no need to keep one book per company – in large groups it is usual to have a single book covering all subsidiaries.

Indeed, there is no legal, practical or security requirement to use a printed form at all; a typed certificate is adequate. As with most documents, security lies in the signatures, not in the fact of whether or not a standard printed form has been used to prepare the certificate. The lay-out of the share certificate shown in Draft Wording 8 would be suitable for copying and word-processing on to the company's printed letter-head.

Corporate shareholders

Where one or more of the shareholders is a company, it may be helpful to give some thought at this time to voting arrangements at share-holders' meetings. A corporate shareholder may vote by proxy, but as a proxy is not normally counted in a quorum this can lead to difficulties. It is therefore better that a corporate shareholder should vote by repre-sentative appointed under section 375 of the Act. Such a representative will be counted in the quorum. To appoint a representative a resolution by the directors of the shareholding company will be required: suitable text is given in Draft Wording 19.

It will not be necessary for the company itself to pass such a resolu-tion, unless of course it is to hold shares in other companies.

Directors' interests

Although the declaration of directors' interests can be deferred until a later board meeting, it is better to deal with it at the outset. A draft resolution will be found in the minutes in Draft Wording 7, but the sub-ject has many facets and has been given fuller treatment in Chapter 6.

After the meeting

The following procedures should be observed:

1 Draft the minutes, using Draft Wording 7 as your model. Show the draft to the chairman for approval. As departure from usual practice, it is preferable (and may be essential if the bank insists) for the minutes of the first formal board meeting to be signed by the chair-man immediately, rather than at the next meting. This is perfectly in order, but it will help to avoid objections if the draft minutes have been handed round during the meeting.
2 Send copies of the typed minutes to each director and copy them into the minute book.
3 Send the relevant documents to the bank:
   • one copy of the bank's own form, properly completed and signed (the duplicate should be retained in the company's files and copied, not pasted, into the minute book);

- a copy of the Memorandum and Articles of Association (the bank will retain this for its own files);
- the original Certificate of Incorporation issued by the Registrar of Companies (which will be returned);
- the cheque(s) received from the shareholder(s) in payment for the shares.

Make a note to ensure that in due course you receive back the Certificate of Incorporation and that you are issued with a cheque-book and a paying-in book.

4 Make a diary note to send to the bank as soon as possible the signatures of any absent directors or other signatories.

5 Work through the minutes to ensure that every decision is implemented or notified to those who must act on it. Thus:

   5.1 If any additional directors have been appointed, they should be notified and asked to sign copies of Form 288a (unless these were signed at the meeting) and the forms should be filed with the Registrar of Companies within 14 days of the meeting.

   5.2 The share certificates, dated and signed, should be sent to the shareholders.

   5.3 The auditors should be notified of their appointment. They will require a photocopy of the Memorandum and Articles of Association and may also ask for a copy of the minutes of the first board meeting.

   5.4 The registers and other statutory books should be prepared, as explained in Chapter 10.

Further formalities

The first board meeting may provide an opportunity to consider what further formalities will be required before the company can commence business. These will depend on the nature of the company's intended activities and the way these are to be carried out. Examples are given below:

1 If an existing business is to be taken over, a transfer of assets and obligations will be necessary. Often a simple 'exchange of letters' will provide an adequate legal contract, but in a complex situation, a formal agreement drafted by lawyers may be required.

2 If employees are to transfer, they must by law be given written notification. Subject to this, transfer of employment (without any change in terms of employment) as part of a transfer of the business will not constitute redundancy and should not give rise to claims from employees. Notice must be given to the PAYE office, but the situation

will normally be regarded as continuous employment, without requiring the submission of P45 forms or similar formalities.

3 Customers and suppliers (including those providing office and other services) should be notified.

4 VAT registration may be required, as may registration under such legislation as the Financial Services Act, the Consumer Credit Act or rules specific to the trade about to be commenced.

5 There will be tax implications, and the first board meeting is not too soon to consider these. The Inland Revenue will usually pick up from Companies House the fact that a new company has been incorporated and will ask for such information as it requires, both for PAYE and for corporation tax purposes.

10 Setting up the Statutory Books

What is required?

As soon as a company has been incorporated, it will need to set up and maintain a number of statutory registers. The minimum, for every new company, would be:

- Minute book;
- Register of members;
- Register of directors and secretaries;
- Register of directors' interests.

According to circumstances a company may also require:

- A separate shareholders' minute book;
- Committee minute books;
- Directors' attendance book (often used but not strictly necessary);
- Register of mortgages and charges;
- Register of debenture holders.

The company will also need to keep proper books of account, but that is a separate specialised subject outside the scope of this guide. Similarly, we are not concerned here with the additional registers that have to be maintained only by a public limited company.

What is the minimum requirement?

Only one book is required for the statutory registers. It may, however, consist of separate volumes for each of the registers listed above (between four and nine volumes in all) or it may be a single, all-purpose volume with sections for each of the registers. It may be a bound book or a loose-leaf binder. Any good law stationer will offer a wide range of pre-printed company registers and minute books, from the very simple to the rather elaborate. The all-purpose volumes may include some sections that will never be required.

Some of the pre-printed registers are very good for their purpose, especially if changes are expected to be minimal. Half an hour with such a register and the minutes of the first board meeting should suffice to meet the necessary regulations simply by filling in the relevant blanks on the pages as appropriate. Subsequent changes must be entered as they occur, but if these are few the book will last for years. If there are more sweeping changes (new shareholders, for example, followed by new directors and registered office), some sections of the book may become uncomfortably full while others remain virtually unused. It may even be necessary to buy a new all-purpose volume and start again, closing off every section of the old book with the note: 'Transferred to new register'.

A convenient alternative for the small company

The pre-printed volumes may be over-elaborate for most small companies – the family business or wholly-owned subsidiary, for example, where few changes are expected. The logical solution (one that has proved highly convenient in practice and which meets all Companies Act requirements) is to use for all purposes just one book with blank pages throughout.

The first page can record the name of the company and (for convenience of future reference) its registered number and the date on which it was incorporated. The next page can be used for the minutes of the first board meeting. Subsequent pages (by far the greater part of the book) can be reserved for minutes – whether of board meetings, shareholders' meetings or committee meetings – which can follow in chronological sequence, regardless of the type of meeting. The last few pages, with suitable headings, can then be laid out as the various registers of members and directors, using the formats illustrated in Draft Wordings 9, 11 and 13.

Objections to a single volume

If a single-volume book is adopted, it may be objected that someone unconnected with the company, who was entitled to inspect certain of the registers, would have access to confidential information contained in a different part of the book. Or there may be 'difficult' shareholders who demand to see the minutes of general (shareholders') meetings in the hope of gaining access to the board minutes, which are confidential and which they are not entitled to see. All this is certainly possible, but in more than 30 years as a secretary of many companies I have never known it to happen in the case of a private company. If callers refused to accept a photocopy of the page they wished to see, I would quickly 'seal off' the confidential pages with adhesive tape – and stand over them while the book was in their hands!

A convenient compromise is to have two volumes, one for board minutes, which are confidential, and one for everything else, which the idly curious can see at Companies House anyway.

Bound book or loose-leaf?

The cheapest form of combined minute book and register is probably a simple A4-size notebook (but with a stitched binding rather than glued, tear-off sheets, although it need not be elaborate or expensive), which can be bought from any good stationers. Short entries can be written up in manuscript. Longer entries, such as board minutes, should be typed on loose sheets of A4, which are then trimmed and pasted on to the pages of the bound book.

Adequate precautions must of course be taken against fraud. Old-fashioned paste yields to judicious damping, and many modern adhesives are surprisingly vulnerable to manipulation with a warm flat-iron. Some procedure for signing or initialling each sheet as soon as it is pasted in is clearly desirable. If possible, the signature should start on the pasted-in sheet and run off to finish on the bound page.

A bound book of this type is cheap and convenient for the very smallest company whose board of directors meets, perhaps, only once a year to consider the annual accounts. If more frequent meetings are expected, the small extra cost of a loose-leaf book with plain pages that can be taken out for typing will soon be repaid by the time saved when making entries in the registers or writing up the minutes.

Objections are sometimes raised on the grounds that section 722(2) of the Act provides that:

> Where any such register, index, minute book or account-ing record is not kept by making entries in a bound book, but by some other means, adequate precautions shall be taken for guarding against falsification and facilitating its discovery.

Precautions against falsification

A small private company need not adopt elaborate precautions against fraud, provided it can be shown that an unauthorised person could not remove or substitute a page. Minutes should certainly be in a book, bound or loose-leaf, and a good-quality loose-leaf book (for example, the sort that requires a winding-key to add or remove a page) is recommended. A pile of sheets is not acceptable, even if punched and secured in a file, unless there are adequate precautions against fraud. For the registers it is arguable that where all the information can be written on a single sheet of paper, that sheet should suffice, but it is obviously preferable that the sheet be bound in with the minute book as explained above.

For 'adequate precautions' in the case of a small company, it would be sufficient to show that the loose-leaf binder was kept in a locked cupboard or filing cabinet, the key being in the custody of a responsible official (such as the company secretary) who would take charge of the book itself whenever it was taken out for use or inspection. As a further safeguard, some company secretaries make a practice of initialling each sheet on the binding edge, where the initials will be hidden once the sheet is inserted in the binder. Minutes should be numbered consecutively through the book rather than starting each meeting at no. 1. As a precaution against anyone using the blank lower portion of the last page to add an item for personal advantage, each set of minutes should conclude with such a phrase as 'That concluded the meeting'. To make it difficult to insert a complete set of minutes of a meeting which was not in fact held, it is usual for the numbered minutes to begin with 'The Chairman signed the minutes of the last meeting held on ...' and to end with 'The next meeting will be held on ...'. Ultimately, however, security rests not in elaborate devices but in the safe custody of the book or register itself.

Information required and how to set it out

The minimum requirements are shown in Draft Wordings 9, 11 and 13. Specimen forms in textbooks and the registers sold by most law stationers are often in columnar form, as if the information required were being entered into a spreadsheet designed so that the columns could be added up! Sometimes registers of members are even more complex, having columns in ledger style with debit on the left and credit on the right (for shares bought and sold), which often need to be ruled off and balanced after every transaction to show the balance of shares held. These elaborate rulings, designed for the larger company, are quite unnecessary and rather cumbersome for a small company where there are only one or two shareholders and no more than three or four directors. The entries required to constitute the registers can more readily be written or typed in a horizontal format. A standardised matrix for the word-processor minimises the work entailed for each entry, dispensing with the need for ruled columns.

Every item should be shown for each director or shareholder, even if there is no useful information to record, but there is no need to follow the wordings slavishly. For example, very few directors will have any relevant 'former names', and rather than writing 'Former names: Nil' it may be better to write 'No former names'.

On the other hand it will occasionally be useful to give just a little more than the statutory minimum. For instance, if a director has changed his or her name, the Act does not require you to show when the name was changed, but there might be advantages in writing: 'Formerly Hans Stavinski (that name disused since 15 September 1989)'. This not only puts the information into perspective but also serves as a reminder that after 15 September 2009 (i.e. after 20 years) there will be no need to refer to the former name in such documents as the annual return.

Register of directors' holdings and interests

It is sometimes wrongly assumed that only companies whose shares are listed on the Stock Exchange require a register of directors' holdings and interests. Such a register must be maintained by every company, public or private, listed or not, including 'family business' companies and wholly-owned subsidiaries. This said, it must be admitted that many private companies will rarely or never have entries to make in that register. In that case the register of directors' holdings and interests need be no more than a short, two-line entry:

Register of Directors' Holdings and Interests

No registrable holdings or interests in securities have been notified.

The register must record for every director – even a director of a wholly-owed subsidiary – his or her holdings or dealings in securities (all classes of shares and also debentures) issued by the company, its holding company, its subsidiaries and any fellow-subsidiary – but not securities of any company which is itself a wholly-owned subsidiary.

The responsibility lies with each director to initiate the procedure by notifying the company in writing of the relevant information as listed below. On receiving such information the company secretary must enter the information in the register, adding the date on which the entry was made. The information must be given by the director at the outset when the company is formed or when he becomes a director, and all changes must be notified within five working days of their occurrence and entered in the register within three working days after receipt of the notification.

For full information, reference may be made to sections 324–328 and schedule 13 of the Act, but for normal circumstances the information to be notified is as follows:

1 The number of shares (and, where relevant, the class of shares) or debentures in which the director or any of his or her family has or has acquired or has disposed of an interest. 'Family' in this context includes the wife or husband of a director and the son or daughter under 18 of a director, including stepchildren and adopted children, but does not include a spouse or child who is also a director of the company.

   Directors are also deemed interested in shares if a company is so interested and they (or their family as defined above) control that company or can exercise one-third or more of the votes.
2 The name of the company that issued the shares or debentures. (Usually this will be the company keeping the register, but it may be the company's holding company, its subsidiary or a fellow-subsidiary.)
3 If (as usually) the interest arises from a contract to buy or sell, the price paid or received.
4 The date of the transaction. (The register must record both this date and the date on which the entry is recorded in the register. Bear in mind the time limits indicated above.)
5 In the case of an option to buy shares, the period for which the option lasts and the exercise price.
6 Optionally, an indication that the director's interest is in some way limited (perhaps because he is a trustee without any beneficial interest in the securities), with a request that this, too, be recorded in the register.
7 A statement that the notice is given in fulfilment of the director's obligation under section 324 of the Companies Act 1985. (This need not be entered in the register.)

The entries for each director must be in chronological order. Moreover, if the directors are not shown in alphabetical order, an index must be provided. For a small company there should be no difficulty in obviating the need for an index by recording the directors in alphabetical order. For the 'family business' company where entries are few an alphabetical list on a single page may be practicable. If entries are more frequent, a separate loose-leaf sheet would be preferable for each director so that these can be rearranged alphabetically if directors change or one director's transactions cover more than one sheet.

The requirements for the register of directors' holdings and interests could vary from the quite simple to the highly complex, according to the size of the company or the circumstances of the transaction. A typical 'family business' company will make one set of entries at the outset and leave them unchanged for many years. A private company (company A) which is a subsidiary of a public company (company B) on the other hand will need to record every dealing by each of company A's directors (and their families) in the shares of company B. If company A is not wholly-owned, then dealings in its own shares must be recorded too. If company B has other subsidiaries – companies C and D, which are not wholly-owned – then the register of company A may need to record all interests and transactions by the directors of company A in the shares and debentures of company A, company B, company C and company D.

In most cases there will be clear advantages in a 'narrative' type of register, so that each entry can meet its own special circumstances. Accordingly, Draft Wordings 12 and 13 illustrate a few typical forms of notification, which can be used to guide directors in fulfilment of their obligations and which can be adapted to suit circumstances.

Conclusion

Once the statutory registers have been set up, they should be kept under lock and key so that no-one can tamper with them. Additions or alterations to any minute book or other register should only be made by or under the authority of the company secretary.

It is usual, with a small company, to keep all the registers and minute books at the registered office. Minutes of general meetings and the register of directors and secretaries must be kept at the registered office. Minutes of board meetings and the register of members may be kept elsewhere, but the register of directors' holdings must be kept at the same place as the register of members.

Inspection is permitted – anyone can see the register of members, the register of directors or the register of directors' holdings. Any shareholder may see the minutes of general meetings but not the minutes of board meetings. There is no legal obligation to disclose board minutes to anyone, but obviously reasonable facilities should be given to the directors.

11 Business Letters and Other Stationery

The 'critical path' when forming a company – the task most likely to delay the start of business – is usually not the incorporation of the company but the printing of stationery. This may not matter greatly with some companies where, for example, most of the business is transacted across a shop counter, but where the company will conduct a large part of its business by correspondence the priority will be obvious.

Business letters and other stationery cannot be printed until after the company is incorporated. This is not just commercial prudence; certain details, such as the registered number, are not available until registration. If the stationery is needed urgently it can be designed, proofed and corrected so that when the last-minute details are available the printer can be instructed to go ahead.

Preliminary considerations

Two questions that need to be addressed initially are:

- whether professional design consultants should be brought in or whether the design can be left to the good taste of the printers – or an in-house computer buff;
- whether the company will be registered for value added tax (VAT).

If the company is to be registered for VAT, all invoices must meet VAT requirements, including (but not limited to) stating the VAT number. Registration is obligatory if turnover exceeds £52,000 a year (at the time of writing) and is optional below this level. Registration is a reasonably quick procedure, but a company cannot be formally registered for VAT (and therefore the VAT registration number will not be available) until after incorporation. A provisional application can be lodged while awaiting incorporation.

A subsidiary can be included in the group VAT registration and have the same number. In some circumstances, however, this may be undesirable. For example, if the subsidiary has a small turnover there may be advantages in keeping it outside the VAT net, and if it is mainly exporting there can be cash-flow advantages in a separate registration so that the export subsidiary can recover tax monthly while other companies in the group pay tax on a three-monthly basis.

Business letters

Company business letters must show:

1 the name of the company, ending with 'Limited' or one of its alternatives;
2 the registered office, which must be identified as such (if only one address is shown the words 'registered office' can appear in small type just above or below it, but if the business address is different it is usually shown at the top, and the registered address, with the words 'registered office', is printed near the foot of the paper);
3 the country where the company is registered – this is denoted as one of the following:
   • Registered in England
   • Registered in England and Wales
   • Registered in Wales
   • Registered in Scotland
   • Registered in Cardiff
   • Registered in Edinburgh
4 the registered number;
5 in the case of a Welsh company that has chosen 'Cyfyngedig' (or 'Cyf.') instead of 'Limited' as the last word of its name, a statement (in English) that it is a limited company;
6 in the case of certain guarantee companies with charitable objects, which may be exempted from using the word 'limited' in their names, a statement that it is a limited company;
7 in the case of a charity whose name does not include the word 'charity' or 'charitable', a statement that it is a charity (similar rules apply to an investment company).

In addition, business letters will usually show:

8 the address for correspondence if it is not the registered office;
9 the telephone number and mobile phone number;
10 the e-mail address, telex number and/or fax number, if any;
11 the general nature of the company's business, unless this is obvious from the name.

Sometimes the VAT registration number is also shown. This is a legal requirement on invoices but not on business letters.

It is no longer necessary to show directors' names on business letters.

However, if one or some directors' names are printed, all must be shown. (This rule does not apply if one director is named only in the body of the letter itself, or if the name is typed below the director's signature.)

Invoices

If the company is registered for VAT its invoices must show:

1 the company name;
2 the company's address (i.e. its business address – it is not necessary to show the registered office here);
3 the VAT registration number;
4 the serial number of the invoice;
5 the date of supply (if a different date is also shown as the date of issue of the invoice, the date of supply must be identified by the words: 'tax point');
6 the type of supply (sale, hire, loan, etc.);
7 a description of the goods or services;
8 the total payable excluding VAT;
9 the rate of VAT;
10 the amount of VAT;
11 the rate of any cash discount offered;
12 the customer's name.

Not all of these details need to be printed – items 5, 7, 8, 10 and 12 (and possibly 6) will obviously be typed in as required. Nevertheless, in view of the relative complexity of the requirements it may be safest to provide a space for every item as a safeguard against omission.

Further details of VAT requirements will be found in Notice 700, *The VAT Guide*, available from HM Customs and Excise (see Directory for details). The guide includes a suggested form of VAT invoice using a commendable economy of wording that can usefully be followed.

Where a company is not registered for VAT, item 1 is the only legal requirement, but items 1, 2, 5, 7, 8 and 12 will probably meet all commercial requirements.

Name of company

In addition to appearing on business letters and invoices, the company's name must be shown:

1 on its cheques (the bank will normally attend to this) and on bills of exchange;
2 on receipts, if issued;
3 outside 'every office or place in which its business is carried on'.

CHAPTER 11

Note the ambiguity of the third requirement. Must the name appear outside 'every office' or only outside those places 'in which its business is carried on'? If the registered office is an address at which the company does not conduct business (for example, the solicitor's office or even the company secretary's residence), does the company's name need to be shown there? The wording of the Companies Act 1985 leaves the matter open to some doubt, but it is usually thought wisest to show the name even if not strictly necessary rather than to risk a penalty for non-compliance.

A Welsh company that uses the word 'Cyfyngedig' (or 'Cyf.') rather than 'Limited' must also state (in English) outside every place where it carries on business that it is a limited company.

What is the meaning of 'outside'? If the company occupies just one or two rooms in a large office block, must the name be displayed outside the building? There may be some doubt, but it is usually thought sufficient for the name to be shown outside the first door a visitor must pass through when entering the company's premises. What if the company conducts the whole of its business in the open air? In unusual circumstances such as these, it is almost certainly sufficient to ensure that anyone dealing with the company sees the company name (possibly on an order form or similar documentation) before concluding any formal dealing with the company.

12 Changes After Incorporation

If a simple company has been set up on the lines already explained, it should be possible to accommodate most developments of the business without needing to make alterations to the formal documentation. But after the company is incorporated an error may be discovered, or there may be second thoughts on some point of detail. From time to time in the life of most companies some change occurs for which it is necessary (or at least prudent) to make corresponding changes in the formal documentation. For a small private company the procedure is quite simple, but it is set out in this chapter for the sake of completeness and to safeguard against overlooking some detail.

What can be changed?

Almost anything can be changed. The exceptions are the registered number, which is given to the company when it is incorporated and which is used throughout its life to distinguish it from any other company, and the country in which the company is registered.

Changes by the board

The following changes can be made by a simple resolution by the board of directors, after which details of the change on the prescribed form must be filed with the Registrar of Companies within 14 days:

- Appointment of an additional director (Form 288a);
- Change of secretary (Forms 288a and 288b must both be completed);
- Change of registered office (Form 287);
- Change of accounting reference date (Form 225(1) or 225(2)).

Fuller details are given later in this chapter.

Changes by the shareholders

The following cannot be changed by the directors; they require a special resolution passed at a meeting of the shareholders:

- the name of the company;
- the Articles of Association;
- the objects clause of the Memorandum.

An issue of new shares also requires the authority of the shareholders, but for this an ordinary resolution is sufficient. (This, too, is explained later.)

Special resolutions

Draft wordings for special resolutions to change the name, the Articles or the objects clause are given in Draft Wording 16. There are three ways in which a special resolution can be passed:

1 If you can secure the signature of every shareholder, the whole procedure can be comprised in a single sheet of paper – a resolution in writing. A suitable draft appears as Draft Wording 14.
2 If you can secure the signature of most, but not quite all, the shareholders, delay can be avoided if the available shareholders sign a waiver of the normal requirement for 21 clear days' notice. A meeting must be held, notice of the meeting must be given and the waiver must be signed by 95 per cent of the shareholders. These shareholders must also hold 95 per cent of the shares.
3 If neither of these alternatives is available, a meeting must be held after 21 clear days' notice has been given. At the meeting the resolution must be passed by a three-fourths majority. Drafts for the notice and minutes of such a meeting are shown as Draft Wordings 15 and 17, respectively.

The requirement for 21 clear days' notice means 21 days excluding the day of the meeting and excluding the day on which the notice is served. There is a trap here. Regulation 115 of Table A provides that if notice is given to a member by post, it is deemed given 48 hours after posting. Thus if notice is posted on Monday it is deemed served on Wednesday and the first 'clear day' is Thursday. The last (twenty-first) clear day will be a Wednesday and the earliest day for holding the meeting will be a Thursday – the same day of the week as the first clear day.

The risk of error will be obvious. If there is no great urgency it may be best to reckon to give a full month's notice.

A three-fourths majority requires that three-fourths of the members voting on the resolution shall vote in favour. If a poll is demanded, votes in favour must represent three-fourths of the total shares in respect of which votes are given. In neither case does the chairman have a casting vote, because an equality of voting indicates that the proposed resolution is lost anyway.

A written resolution for a special resolution could take the form of a single typed sheet of paper. If a loose-leaf minute book is used, a sheet could be taken from that book. It is obviously convenient if every shareholder signs on the same sheet of paper, but if necessary some of the shareholders could sign on separate copies, provided every shareholder signs and provided the actual resolution is worded identically on all the copies.

When the resolution in writing has been drafted, typed and signed by every shareholder, it should be dated with the date of the last signature and then pasted or bound into the minute book. Since it has been signed by every shareholder, it does not need the signature of the chairman at the next board meeting to authenticate it, but it is usual (and could be a precaution against fraud or oversight) to refer to it in the minutes of the next board meeting on the following lines:

> The board noted the terms of the special resolution in writing, signed by all the shareholders and dated...

Filing

When the resolution has been passed, by whichever method, a copy should be filed with Companies House. The correct layout is shown as Draft Wording 18. This document should be authenticated by the signature of the secretary (or, if the secretary is not available, by a director) and sent to Companies House to arrive within 15 days of the date of the resolution.

If the resolution alters the Articles or the objects clause of the Memorandum, a complete copy of the document as amended must be prepared and filed at the same time as the resolution itself. A change in the name of the company is not regarded for this purpose as a change in the Memorandum or Articles.

No fee is payable except in the case of a resolution to change the company's name, when the fee is £10, or £100 for same-day registration.

If the resolution – for instance, to adopt a complete new set of Articles rather than simply to amend details – refers to another document ('the document annexed hereto and signed for purposes of identification by...'), a copy of that document should be attached. It should be authenticated by the same signature as that which authenticated the resolution, written beneath such words as:

> This is the document referred to in the special resolution of
> ABC Limited dated ...

How soon does the change take effect?

An alteration to the Articles or to the objects clause of the Memorandum takes effect as soon as it is signed and dated – even though
it has not yet been filed at Companies House. A resolution to change
the company's name does not become effective until the date shown on
the new 'Certificate of Incorporation on Change of Name' issued by
Companies House.

Change of name

The procedure for changing a company's name is similar to that for
changing the Articles, except for the £10 fee payable on filing the
special resolution. The change becomes effective when Companies
House issues a new 'Certificate of Incorporation on Change of Name'.
A change of name will entail reprinting stationery and altering the
name outside all offices. See Checklist F for points to watch.

If, for commercial reasons or to match other changes elsewhere, you
wish the change of name to take effect on a particular date you should
write to or telephone Companies House before passing the special resolution to agree a timetable. You should refer to this in a covering letter,
reminding them of the agreed date, when you send the special resolution for filing.

As an alternative, Companies House offers a premium service. If the
special resolution is delivered to Companies House before 3.00 pm
and a fee of £100.00 instead of £10.00 is paid, the Certificate of Incorporation on Change of Name can be issued at once, dated that day.

Increase in share capital

There are two stages for an increase in the issued capital of the company. First, the members (shareholders) must authorise the directors to
make the issue; then the directors invite applications for shares and
allot them.

Before calling the general (shareholders') meeting, you must consider
the following points:

1 Power to increase the share capital must be included in the Articles
   (e.g. regulation 32 of Table A or its equivalent). If that power is not

given in the Articles, they must be amended at the meeting by a special resolution.

2 The proposed increase must be within the company's *authorised* capital – i.e. there must be sufficient capital authorised but un-issued to accommodate the proposed new issue. If there is not, the authorised capital must be increased by ordinary resolution passed at the general meeting. The procedure is similar to that for a special resolution, except that 14 clear days' notice and a simple majority (i.e. more that half) are sufficient.

3 The shareholders must, within the previous five years, have authorised the board to allot the shares. This authority may be given by the Articles (though it is not given by Table A) or it may have been given on a previous occasion; but if neither applies, or if the authority has expired (being more than five years old), another ordinary resolution will be required.

4 Unless the new shares are to be issued in proportion to existing holdings, the basis for allotment must be authorised by the shareholders by special resolution.

5 If the new shares are to be issued on special terms – i.e. if they are a new *class* of share – the special rights and duties attaching to the shares must be specifically authorised by the shareholders in general meeting. This is often done by a special resolution to insert an additional regulation in the Articles of Association, as it provides a permanent record. However, an ordinary resolution to authorise the terms of the issue without altering the Articles is sufficient if that is preferred.

The first step therefore is for the directors to instruct the secretary to call a general (shareholders') meeting to cover any of these five points where authority is lacking. With a small private company it is not unusual when sending out the call notices to invite the shareholders at the same time to apply for shares, normally in proportion to the shares already held and subject to the resolutions being duly passed. Immediately after the general meeting a board meeting can be held to allot the shares formally. Share certificates can then be issued. With a small company, it is unnecessary to issue allotment letters. Whether it would be sensible to delay the issue of certificates until cheques have been cleared through the company's bank account is a matter for judgment, but with many small companies this precaution is perhaps unnecessary.

Any special resolution(s) passed at the general meeting and also the ordinary resolution to increase the authorised capital must be filed at Companies House within 14 days of the meeting, and a return of allotments on Form 88(2) must be filed within one month after the shares are allotted. The return of allotments lists the names and addresses of the new shareholders and shows the number of the shares allotted. All these documents can be sent to Companies House at the same time.

Appointment of an additional director

The appointment of an additional director (within any maximum prescribed by the Articles) can be effected in any manner prescribed by the Articles. Usually a new director is appointed 'to fill a casual vacancy' by a resolution at a board meeting, which might be worded: '…that Mr __ be and is hereby appointed an additional director of the company.' This style may sound awkward, but the usage is well established. The words 'be and is hereby' make it clear that the appointment has been made and is effective from the moment the resolution is passed.

Following the appointment, Form 288a, signed by the new director and by the company secretary, must be filed at Companies House within 14 days. A number of consequential points may arise, such as arranging for the new director to sign cheques, and these are indicated in Checklist D.

Resignation of a director

Removal of a director can be difficult. The procedure is set out in the next section, but it is in every way better to ask the director to resign. A director may resign by writing a letter to that effect, sending it to the company secretary. The resignation will take effect on the date stated in the letter, or if no date is stated as soon as the letter reaches the company. It is customary for the secretary (or possibly the chairman) to report the resignation at the next board meeting so that it may be recorded in the minutes.

Alternatively, the director may resign orally. Provided this is done at a board meeting and the remaining directors thereupon resolve to accept the resignation, a binding contract has been created and the resignation will take immediate effect. This oral resignation will be as valid as a written one even though the company's Articles (as in regulation 81(d) of Table A, read in conjunction with regulation 111) appear to require a written resignation.

Form 288b recording the change must be filed with the Registrar of Companies within 14 days of the resignation taking effect.

Removal of a director

Occasionally the board (or the shareholders) may wish to remove a director who refuses to resign. Unless there are unusual provisions in the company's Articles a director cannot be removed by the remaining directors, only by the shareholders. Irrespective of the Articles, the shareholders will always have the power to remove a director under section 303(1) of the Act. However, this procedure should only be undertaken with great care and meticulous attention to detail. Even a minor irregularity may entitle a disgruntled director to claim that he has not effectively been removed. In any case he may be able to claim damages for loss of office. The procedure is set out in detail in Checklist E.

Change of secretary

Such problems do not arise with a change of company secretary. If a change is desired company secretaries will usually be asked to resign, but if they refuse to do so the board can always remove them by a board resolution and appoint another in the same way. (The removed secretary will usually have a claim for damages for loss of office and perhaps also for unfair dismissal, but that is another matter.) The procedure is similar to that for the resignation of a director, and Checklist E may be used, subject to minor details.

Several simultaneous changes

Where several changes of directors or secretary (or both) are made at the same time, the company must ensure that it has at all times at least one secretary and at least one director who is not the same person as the secretary. In most cases this will present no difficulty, but if the board of directors is to be completely replaced (for example, following a change in ownership) it is important to make the new appointments before accepting the resignations of the outgoing directors, lest you reach a stage where there is no board to make the new appointments! A useful safeguard is for the outgoing director(s) to word their resignations: '... with effect at the conclusion of the board meeting to be held on [date].'

Change of registered office

A change in the registered office calls for no more than a simple board resolution and filing Form 287. Consequential procedures will be obvious. The company's letterhead will need to be reprinted and you should not forget to display the company name outside the new office.

Change in accounting reference date

The accounting reference date is fixed automatically at the outset as the anniversary of the last date of the month in which the company was incorporated. Any subsequent change can be made by a simple board resolution and filed on Form 225.

The points to be considered in deciding the new accounting reference date are set out in Chapter 7, but when a change is being contemplated there are one or two special details to bear in mind.

An alteration may either extend or shorten the accounting period, but it must not extend it beyond 18 months and must not extend it more than once in any five years. Normally a change may be made only *during* the accounting period which is to be shortened or lengthened. If the date up to which the accounts should have been made has already passed, the accounts must be prepared and filed as at that date and any change will take effect only from the beginning of the next accounting period. In all these circumstances Form 225 is appropriate.

To this last point there is, however, one exception. If a subsidiary intends to change its accounting reference date so that it coincides with that of its parent company, notice may be given during the year or it may be given after the old accounting reference date has passed, provided the last date for delivering copies of the accounts to the Registrar of Companies has not also passed.

Change of shareholder – share transfer

A change of shareholder may arise as a 'transmission' – an involuntary change arising, for example, from the death of a shareholder or from a voluntary decision to transfer ownership to some other person.

A voluntary transfer requires a Stock Transfer Form, a specimen of which is shown as Draft Wording 21. This form is not a form prescribed under the Companies Acts and cannot be supplied by Companies House, but it may be obtained for a modest charge from any good stationer (see under 'law stationers' or 'legal stationers' in your local *Yellow Pages*). The transfer form used for Stock Exchange transactions should not be used, as it will not provide all the information required.

For an unlimited company, use a Common Form of Transfer (obtainable from the same source). The main difference is that the transferee must also sign the form to indicate his acceptance of unlimited liability.

Unless the transfer can be certified as exempt, as explained below, stamp duty must be paid and impressed on the form itself at one of the Inland Revenue Stamp Offices (listed in the Directory) before the transfer can be registered by the company.

When the stock transfer form, completed, signed and stamped (or certified exempt), is presented to the company with the relevant share certificate, it should be presented to a meeting of the directors. Private companies may have the power to decline to register a transfer of shares to a person of whom the board do not approve, but only if this is explicitly spelled out in the Articles of Association. If all is in order, the board should resolve to approve the transfer and the company secretary should make entries in the register of members to give it effect. The old share certificate should be cancelled and a new one sent to the new shareholder. If the number of shares transferred is smaller than the number covered by the accompanying certificate, a 'balance certificate' should also be prepared for the number of shares not transferred.

Stamp duty on share transfers

Stamp duty on share transfers is calculated as 0.5 per cent of the price paid for the shares, rounded up to the nearest £5.00 and is subject to a minimum of £5.00. Thus, if £12,345.67 is paid for a block of shares, 0.5 per cent is £61.73, but the stamp duty is rounded up to £65.00. If nothing is paid for the shares in money or in money's worth – say, because the shares are transferred as a gift or to a trustee – either the transfer may rank for a nominal duty of £5.00 or it may be completely exempt.

It is the responsibility of the secretary of the company whose shares are being transferred to ensure that the proper stamp duty has been paid or that the exemption certificate has been properly signed. Otherwise he or she will be personally liable for any stamp duty unpaid – and for hefty penalties as well!

Exemption or a reduced rate of duty is claimed by completing one of the two forms of certificate printed on the back of the stock transfer form. Where complete exemption is claimed, the upper certificate should be completed; where the transfer is subject only to £5.00 nominal duty, the lower form. Each certificate lists the circumstances to which it applies and the appropriate category must be indicated by inserting the relevant number or letter in the appropriate place on the certificate before it is signed.

The most usual cases are transfers arising from a will or intestacy or where the shares are a gift. Where shares pass as a gift they are exempt because they fall within class L on the back of the form ('voluntary dispositions *inter vivos*') and the relevant certificate must be completed and signed accordingly. It should be noted, however, that *ad valorem* stamp duty is always payable where money (or other value) is paid for the shares, even on transfers between husband and wife.

The exemption certificate, like the transfer itself, must be signed by the transferor and dated. Where the transferor is a company the transfer itself will normally be signed on behalf of the company by a director and the secretary, but the signature of the company secretary alone is sufficient on the stamp duty certificate. If exemption applies, the form does not need to be sent to the Stamp Duty Office.

Transmission

On the death of a shareholder who left a will, the executors should apply for probate. If the deceased did not leave a will, the next-of-kin should apply for letters of administration. In either case the legal personal representatives (executors or administrators) should present the document to the company, which must then annotate the register of members to the effect that the member is deceased and that the persons named in the document are the legal personal representatives. Once a copy has been made for the company's records, the document should be returned to the legal personal representatives. At the same time they can be asked to complete either a letter of request to have the shares registered in their own names or a stock transfer form to have the shares transferred to someone else – probably the legatee(s) entitled under the terms of the will. A form of letter of request is shown as Draft Wording 20. When the form has been completed, signed by all the executors or administrators and presented to the company, the secretary should deal with it in the same way as a share transfer. The 'letter of request' does not attract stamp duty.

Conclusion

All this may seem troublesome, but rarely should any procedure described in this chapter be necessary at the time of formation of a company. Even afterwards, most small private companies will only occasionally need to change anything in the formal constitution. If it proves otherwise, this chapter will be a useful point of reference – and it will be well to remember that efficient handling of any situation that arises is an invaluable test of the company secretary's competence.

Timetables and Checklists

Checklist A – Company Formation

✱✱ Limited

	Refer to	Target completion date
1 Select name: **1.1** Check that it is not already in use by an existing company. **1.2** Check whether it includes 'sensitive' words. **1.3** If it does, apply for permission. **1.4** Check that it does not include 'Limited', etc., except as the last word, and that it does not imply government/local government connections.	Chapter 2 and Appendix	
2 Design stationery (proofs only): **2.1** letterheads; **2.2** invoices, etc.	Chapter 11	
3 Draft: **3.1** Memorandum of Association; **3.2** Articles of Association.	Chapter 3; Draft 1 or 2 Chapter 4; Drafts 4, 5	
4 Prepare forms for filing: **4.1** Form 10 (registered office, directors, secretary); **4.2** Form 12 (statutory declaration of compliance); **4.3** Form 225 (accounting reference date).	Chapter 8; Checklist C	
5 • Meet to sign all documents. • Secretary and every director to attend. • Prepare checklist of signatures required.	Chapter 8	

CHECKLIST A

	Refer to	Target completion date
6 Send all documents to Registrar of Companies: **6.1** Memorandum and Articles (3 above); **6.2** Forms 10, 12 and 225 (4 above); **6.3** £20 registration fee (£100 for same-day registration).	Chapter 8	
7 Decide on bankers and obtain printed form to open account(s).	Chapter 9	
8 Await Certificate of Incorporation.		
9 Order stationery, etc.	Chapter 11	

10 First board meeting:
• Receive:
  • Certificate of Incorporation;
  • Memorandum and Articles.
• Appoint:
  • Chairman;
  • Secretary;
  • Auditors.
• Sign first share certificates.
• Open bank account.
• Determine accounting reference date.
• Directors' declaration of interests.
• Commercial business as appropriate.
	Chapter 9
	
	Draft 8
	
	Chapter 7
	
	Chapter 6	

11 Open statutory registers: • Register of Members; • Register of Directors and Secretaries; • Register of Directors' Holdings; • Minute book(s).	Chapter 10 Draft 9 Draft 11 Draft 13	

CHECKLIST A

Checklist B – Taking Instructions to Form a Company

The following information is required:

Name of company
• Alternative names in case the first choice is not available.

Directors
• Full names.
• Any former names (unless disused for 20 years).
• Nationality.
• Usual residential address (a business address is not sufficient).
• Date of birth.
• Business occupation.
• Other directorships, including directorships held at any time during the preceding five years. Overseas companies and wholly-owned subsidiaries within the same group may be omitted. (Although it is not strictly necessary to include them, the dates of appointment to and resignation from former directorships will be found useful.)

In England, any person may be appointed a director of a private company. There are no age limits, although there may be practical problems if a very young person is appointed. In Scotland there is a minimum age of 16. Directors need not have British nationality, but those whose nationality is outside the European Union may be subject to employment restrictions. Enquiry can be made of the Home Office Immigration and Nationality Department (see Directory).

Company secretary
• Full name.
• Any former names (unless disused for 20 years).
• Usual residential address (not business address).

A company needs only one director and one secretary. The secretary can also be a director, but a sole director cannot also be the secretary – at least two persons are always required.

Registered office
The registered office is where the minute books and other statutory records are kept and where writs may be served on the company. It will normally be the office of the company secretary but could be the address of the company's lawyers or auditors.

Other details

- Accounting reference date (see Chapter 7).
- Issued share capital.
- Purpose of the company and any other information necessary to draft the Memorandum and Articles of Association (see Chapters 3 and 4).
- Whether there exists any partnership, shareholders' or joint venture agreement which is to form the basis for the new company; or whether there are any other documents, such as correspondence, board minutes or a record of discussions.
- Whether a shareholders' agreement has been prepared.
  - If so, ask for a copy.
  - If not, ask if one should be prepared (see Chapter 5).

Checklist C – Prescribed Form 10 (page 1)

Please complete in typescript, or in bold black capitals.
CHFP087

10

First directors and secretary and intended situation of registered office

Notes on completion appear on final page

Company Name in full

Proposed Registered Office

(PO Box numbers only, are not acceptable)

Post town

County / Region   Postcode

If the memorandum is delivered by an agent for the subscriber(s) of the memorandum mark the box opposite and give the agent's name and address.

Agent's Name

Address

Post town

County / Region   Postcode

Number of continuation sheets attached

Please give the name, address, telephone number and, if available, a DX number and Exchange of the person Companies House should contact if there is any query.

Tel

DX number   DX exchange

Companies House receipt date barcode

When you have completed and signed the form please send it to the Registrar of Companies at:
Companies House, Crown Way, Cardiff, CF14 3UZ   DX 33050 Cardiff
for companies registered in England and Wales
or

Form revised July 1998

Companies House, 37 Castle Terrace, Edinburgh, EH1 2EB
for companies registered in Scotland   **DX 235 Edinburgh**

Checklist C (*cont.*) – Prescribed Form 10 (page 2)

Company Secretary (see notes 1-5)

Company name		

NAME *Style / Title* | | *Honours etc* |

* Voluntary details

Forename(s)

Surname

Previous forename(s)

Previous surname(s)

Address

Usual residential address
For a corporation, give the
registered or principal office
address.

Post town

County / Region | | Postcode |

Country

I consent to act as secretary of the company named on page 1

Consent signature | | **Date** |

Directors (see notes 1-5)

Please list directors in alphabetical order

NAME *Style / Title* | | *Honours etc* |

Forename(s)

Surname

Previous forename(s)

Previous surname(s)

Address

Usual residential address
For a corporation, give the
registered or principal office
address.

Post town

County / Region | | Postcode |

Country

Day Month Year

Date of birth | | **Nationality** |

Business occupation

Other directorships

I consent to act as director of the company named on page 1

Consent signature | | **Date** |

CHECKLIST C

Checklist C (*cont.*) – Prescribed Form 10 (page 3)

Directors (continued)   (see notes 1-5)

	NAME	*Style / Title		*Honours etc	

* Voluntary details   Forename(s)

Surname

Previous forename(s)

Previous surname(s)

Address

Usual residential address
For a corporation, give the
registered or principal office
address.

Post town

County / Region   Postcode

Country

Day   Month   Year

Date of birth   Nationality

Business occupation

Other directorships

I consent to act as director of the company named on page 1

Consent signature   Date

SPECIMEN

This section must be signed by
Either

an agent on behalf
of all subscribers   **Signed**   **Date**

Or the subscribers   **Signed**   **Date**

(*i.e those who signed
as members on the*   **Signed**   **Date**
*memorandum of
association).*   **Signed**   **Date**

Signed   **Date**

Signed   **Date**

Signed   **Date**

CHECKLIST C

Checklist C (*cont.*) – Prescribed Form 10 (page 4)

Notes

1. Show for an individual the full forename(s) NOT INITIALS and surname together with any previous forename(s) or surname(s).

    If the director or secretary is a corporation or Scottish firm - show the corporate or firm name on the surname line.

    Give previous forename(s) or surname(s) except that:

    - for a married woman, the name by which she was known before marriage need not be given,

    - names not used since the age of 18 or for at least 20 years need not be given.

    A peer, or an individual known by a title, may state the title instead of or in addition to the forename(s) and surname and need not give the name by which that person was known before he or she adopted the title or succeeded to it.

    Address:

    Give the usual residential address.

    In the case of a corporation or Scottish firm give the registered or principal office.

    Subscribers:

    The form must be signed personally either by the subscriber(s) or by a person or persons authorised to sign on behalf of the subscriber(s).

2. Directors known by another description:

    - A director includes any person who occupies that position even if called by a different name, for example, governor, member of council.

3. Directors details:

    - Show for each individual director the director's date of birth, business occupation and nationality. **The date of birth must be given for every individual director.**

4. Other directorships:

    - Give the name of every company of which the person concerned is a director or has been a director at any time in the past 5 years. You may exclude a company which either **is or at all times during the past 5 years,** when the person was a director, **was**:

    - dormant,

    - a parent company which wholly owned the company making the return,

    - a wholly owned subsidiary of the company making the return, or

    - another wholly owned subsidiary of the same parent company.

    If there is insufficient space on the form for other directorships you may use a separate sheet of paper, which should include the company's number and the full name of the director.

5. Use Form 10 continuation sheets or photocopies of page 2 to provide details of joint secretaries or additional directors.

CHECKLIST C

Checklist C (*cont.*) – Prescribed Form 12

12

Please complete in typescript, or in bold black capitals.

CHFP087

Declaration on application for registration

Company Name in full

I,

of

† Please delete as appropriate.

do solemnly and sincerely declare that I am a † [Solicitor engaged in the formation of the company][person named as director or secretary of the company in the statement delivered to the Registrar under section 10 of the Companies Act 1985] and that all the requirements of the Companies Act 1985 in respect of the registration of the above company and of matters precedent and incidental to it have been complied with.

And I make this solemn Declaration conscientiously believing the same to be true and by virtue of the Statutory Declarations Act 1835.

Declarant's signature

Declared at

Day   Month   Year

On

❶ Please print name.

before me ❶

Signed

Date

† A Commissioner for Oaths or Notary Public or Justice of the Peace or Solicitor

Please give the name, address, telephone number and, if available, a DX number and Exchange of the person Companies House should contact if there is any query.

Tel

DX number   DX exchange

Companies House receipt date barcode

When you have completed and signed the form please send it to the Registrar of Companies at:

Companies House, Crown Way, Cardiff, CF14 3UZ   **DX 33050 Cardiff**
for companies registered in England and Wales

or

Form revised June 1998

Companies House, 37 Castle Terrace, Edinburgh, EH1 2EB
for companies registered in Scotland   **DX 235 Edinburgh**

SPECIMEN

CHECKLIST C

Checklist C (*cont.*) – Prescribed Form 225

225

ICSA

Change of accounting reference date

*Please complete in typescript,
or in bold black capitals*
CHFP087

Company Number

Company Name in Full

	Day	Month	Year
The accounting reference period ending			

	Day	Month	Year
is shortened/extended† so as to end on			

NOTES

You may use this form to change the accounting date relating to either the current or the immediately previous accounting period.

a. You **may not** change a period for which the accounts are already overdue.

b. You **may not** extend a period beyond 18 months unless the company is subject to an administration order.

c. You **may not** extend periods more than once in five years unless:

1. the company is subject to an administration order, or

2. you have the specific approval of the Secretary of State, (please enclose a copy), or

3. you are extending the company's accounting reference period to align with that of a parent or subsidiary undertaking established in the European Economic Area, or

4. the form is being submitted by an oversea company.

Subsequent periods will end on the same day and month in future years.

If extending more than once in five years, please indicate in the box the number of the provision listed in note c. on which you are relying.

SPECIMEN

Signed

Date

† Please delete as appropriate

† a director / secretary / administrator / administrative receiver / receiver and manager / receiver (Scotland) / person authorised on behalf of an oversea company

Please give the name, address, telephone number, and if available, a DX number and Exchange, for the person Companies House should contact if there is any query

Tel

DX number   DX exchange

Companies House receipt date barcode

When you have completed and signed the form please send it to the Registrar of Companies at:

Companies House, Crown Way, Cardiff, CF14 3UZ   DX 33050 Cardiff
for companies registered in England and Wales

or

Companies House, 37 Castle Terrace, Edinburgh, EH1 2EB
for companies registered in Scotland   **DX 235 Edinburgh**

Form revised July 1998

CHECKLIST C

Checklist C (*cont.*) – Prescribed Form 287

287

ICSA PUBLISHING

Please complete in typescript,
or in bold black capitals.
CHFP087

Change in situation or address of Registered Office

Company Number

Company Name in full

New situation of registered office

NOTE:

The change in the
situation of the
registered office does
not take effect until the
Registrar has registered
this notice.

For 14 days beginning
with the date that a
change of registered
office is registered, a
person may validly serve
any document on the
company at its previous
registered office.

PO Box numbers only
are not acceptable.

Address

Post town

County / Region   Postcode

SPECIMEN

Signed   **Date**

† *Please delete as appropriate.*

† a director / secretary / administrator / administrative receiver / liquidator / receiver manager / receiver

Please give the name, address,
telephone number and, if available,
a DX number and Exchange of
the person Companies House should
contact if there is any query.

Tel

DX number   DX exchange

Companies House receipt date barcode

When you have completed and signed the form please send it to the
Registrar of Companies at:
Companies House, Crown Way, Cardiff, CF14 3UZ   DX 33050 Cardiff
for companies registered in England and Wales
or
Companies House, 37 Castle Terrace, Edinburgh, EH1 2EB
for companies registered in Scotland   **DX 235 Edinburgh**

Form revised June 1998

CHECKLIST C

Checklist C (*cont.*) – Prescribed Form 288a (page 1)

288a

APPOINTMENT of director or secretary
(NOT for resignation (use Form 288b) or change of particulars (use Form 288c))

Please complete in typescript, or in bold black capitals.
CHFP087

Company Number

Company Name in full

	Day	Month	Year		Day	Month	Year
Date of appointment				†Date of Birth			

Appointment form

Notes on completion appear on reverse.

Appointment as director | as secretary | *Please mark the appropriate box. If appointment is as a director and secretary mark both boxes.*

NAME
*Style / Title | †Honours etc
Forename(s)
Surname
Previous Forename(s) | Previous Surname(s)

Usual residential address
Post town | Postcode
County / Region | Country
†Nationality | †Business occupation
†Other directorships (additional space overleaf)

Consent signature
I consent to act as ** director / secretary of the above named company

Date

* Voluntary details.
† Directors only.
**Delete as appropriate

A director, secretary etc must sign the form below.

Signed | Date

(**a director / secretary / administrator / administrative receiver / receiver manager / receiver)

Please give the name, address, telephone number and, if available, a DX number and Exchange of the person Companies House should contact if there is any query.

Tel

DX number | DX exchange

Companies House receipt date barcode

When you have completed and signed the form please send it to the Registrar of Companies at:
Companies House, Crown Way, Cardiff, CF14 3UZ DX 33050 Cardiff
for companies registered in England and Wales **or**
Companies House, 37 Castle Terrace, Edinburgh, EH1 2EB
for companies registered in Scotland DX 235 Edinburgh

Form revised July 1998

SPECIMEN

CHECKLIST C

Checklist C (*cont.*) – Prescribed Form 288a (page 2)

Company Number

† Directors only.

†Other directorships

NOTES

Show the full forenames, NOT INITIALS. If the director or secretary is a corporation or Scottish firm, show the name on surname line and registered or principal office on the usual residential line.

Give previous forenames or surname(s) except:
- for a married woman, the name by which she was known before marriage need not be given.
- for names not used since the age of 18 or for at least 20 years

A peer or individual known by a title may state the title instead of or in addition to the forenames and surname and need not give the name by which that person was known before he or she adopted the title or succeeded to it.

Other directorships.

Give the name of every company incorporated in Great Britain of which the person concerned is a director or has been a director at any time in the past five years.

You may exclude a company which either is, or at all times during the past five years when the person concerned was a director, was
- dormant
- a parent company which wholly owned the company making the return, or
- another wholly owned subsidiary of the same parent company.

SPECIMEN

Checklist C (*cont.*) – Prescribed Form 288b

288b

ICSA

Please complete in typescript, or in bold black capitals.
CHFP087

Terminating appointment as director or secretary
(NOT for appointment (use Form 288a) or change of particulars (use Form 288c))

Company Number

Company Name in full

Date of termination of appointment

Day Month Year

as director   as secretary   *Please mark the appropriate box. If terminating appointment as a director and secretary mark both boxes.*

NAME   *Style / Title*   *Honours etc*

Please insert details as previously notified to Companies House.

Forename(s)

Surname

†Date of Birth   Day Month Year

SPECIMEN

A serving director, secretary etc must sign the form below.

Signed   **Date**

* Voluntary details.
† Directors only.
** Delete as appropriate

(** serving director / secretary / administrator / administrative receiver / receiver manager / receiver)

Please give the name, address, telephone number and, if available, a DX number and Exchange of the person Companies House should contact if there is any query.

Tel

DX number   DX exchange

Companies House receipt date barcode

When you have completed and signed the form please send it to the Registrar of Companies at:
Companies House, Crown Way, Cardiff, CF14 3UZ   DX 33050 Cardiff
for companies registered in England and Wales   **or**
Companies House, 37 Castle Terrace, Edinburgh, EH1 2EB
for companies registered in Scotland   **DX 235 Edinburgh**

Form revised 1999

CHECKLIST C

Checklist C (*cont.*) – Prescribed Form 288c

288c

ICSA

Please complete in typescript, or in bold black capitals.

CHFP087

CHANGE OF PARTICULARS for director or secretary*(NOT for appointment (use Form 288a) or resignation (use Form 288b))*

Company Number

Company Name in full

Changes of particulars form — *Complete in all cases*

Date of change of particulars — Day Month Year

Name — *Style / Title — *Honours etc

Forename(s)

Surname

† Date of Birth — Day Month Year

Change of name *(enter new name)* Forename(s)

Surname

Change of usual residential address *(enter new address)*

Post town

County / Region — Postcode

Country

Other change *(please specify)*

A serving director, secretary etc must sign the form below.

* Voluntary details.
† Directors only.
**Delete as appropriate.

Signed — **Date**

(** director / secretary / administrator / administrative receiver / receiver manager / receiver)

Please give the name, address, telephone number and, if available, a DX number and Exchange of the person Companies House should contact if there is any query.

Tel

DX number — DX exchange

Companies House receipt date barcode

When you have completed and signed the form please send it to the Registrar of Companies at:
Companies House, Crown Way, Cardiff, CF14 3UZ — **DX 33050 Cardiff**
for companies registered in England and Wales — **or**
Companies House, 37 Castle Terrace, Edinburgh, EH1 2EB
for companies registered in Scotland — **DX 235 Edinburgh**

Form revised July 1998

CHECKLIST C

SPECIMEN

Checklist D – Appointment of an Additional Director

1 Preliminaries

1.1 Secure the agreement in principle of the existing directors and/or the shareholders.

1.2 Ask the proposed director whether he or she is willing to serve.

1.3 If so, ask for information to complete Form 288a and the Register of Directors' Holdings and Interests.

1.4 Complete Form 288a and ask the proposed director to sign it.

1.5 If the new director is to sign cheques etc., ask for a specimen signature (see Chapter 9).

1.6 Subject to the agreement of existing directors, invite the proposed director to attend the next board meeting.

2 Appointment

Board meeting to resolve: 'That Mr _____ be and is hereby appointed an additional director of the company.'

3 Follow-up

3.1 Enter the details in the Register of Directors and in the Register of Directors' Holdings and Interests.

3.2 File at Companies House Form 288a, signed by the new director and the secretary.

3.3 If the new director is to sign cheques, send a certified copy of the board resolution with specimen signature to the bank.

3.4 Enter the new director on the payroll for fees or other emoluments.

Checklist E – Removal of a Director

Unless the company's articles of association include unusual provisions, a director can only be removed from office by the shareholders, who must adopt the 'special notice' procedure.

1 One of the shareholders (possibly, but not necessarily, a director) must give written notice to the company that he or she will propose at the next shareholders' meeting: 'That Mr _____ be and is hereby removed from the office of director of the company.'

2 The company secretary must immediately send a copy of this notice to the director concerned.

3 The director may then write to the company, at reasonable length, in regard to the matter and ask that copies of these representations be sent to all shareholders.

4 The board must resolve to call a shareholders' meeting to consider the proposal.

5 The company secretary, being so authorised by the board, must call a meeting of shareholders, giving 21 clear days' notice. The notice of the meeting must be sent to every shareholder, to the auditors and to the director who is to be removed and must set out:

5.1 the usual details (date, time and place) of the meeting;

5.2 the resolution to be proposed, worded exactly as the notice given under 1 above;

5.3 the fact that the director concerned has made written representations (3 above) if he has in fact done so;

5.4 the usual note that a member may appoint a proxy.

5.5 If 5.3 applies, a copy of the communication from the director must be enclosed with the notice. In counting 'clear days', exclude the day of the meeting and also the day on which the notice is deemed served. (Articles typically provide that notice is deemed served 48 hours after it is posted.)

It would be wise to allow 28 clear days between the date the company received notice under 1 above and the date of the meeting. This is not essential, as section 379(3) of the Act makes clear, but for the sake of a few days' delay it may avoid argument as to the validity of the notice.

6 If representations under 3 above are received too late for enclosure with the notice of the meeting, they must nevertheless be sent to every shareholder if there is time; and if there is not, the director may require that they be read out at the meeting.

7 The meeting must be held (with due attention to the usual formalities, such as quorum and ensuring the correct person is in the chair) and the proposition moved (usually, but not necessarily, by the shareholder who gave notice under 1 above) in the precise words of the special notice. Opportunity must be given for discussion, and in particular the director must be given reasonable opportunity to speak.

8 After discussion the chairman must put the question to the vote. A simple majority of the shareholders (not the directors) will suffice to pass the resolution. Directors may vote if they are also shareholders but not otherwise. In the event of an equality of votes the chairman will, subject to the articles, have a casting vote, whether or not he or she is a shareholder. The chairman will then formally announce that the resolution is (or is not) carried.

9 If the resolution is carried, all consequential items must be attended to. The checklist for the appointment of a director (Checklist D) may provide useful reminders, but in most cases the requirements will be to:

9.1 enter the termination, with the date, in the Register of Directors and in the Register of Directors' Holdings and Interests;

9.2 file Form 288b recording the termination with the Registrar of Companies;

9.3 notify the bank if the effect of the termination is to terminate also the director's power to sign cheques;

9.4 ensure that any company property held by the director is returned, or other arrangements are made;

9.5 pay directors' fees or other emoluments up to the date of termination and ensure that automatic regular payments are discontinued.

Auditors

The procedure for the removal of an auditor is similar, except that none of the items listed under 9 above will apply. Nevertheless, it is necessary to ensure that all the company's papers and records have been returned.

CHECKLIST E

Checklist F – Changing a Company Name

Old name: * * **Limited**

New name: * * **Limited**

	Refer to	Target completion date

1 Select new name:
  1.1 Check that it is not already in use by an existing company, etc.
  1.2 Check whether it includes 'sensitive' words.
  1.3 If it does, apply for permission.
  1.4 Check that it does not include 'Limited', etc., except as the last word, and that it does not imply government or local government connections.
	Chapter 2 and Appendix	

2 Design new stationery (proofs only at this stage):
  2.1 letterheads;
  2.2 invoices, etc.;
  2.3 cheques.
	Chapter 11	

3 Board meeting to resolve to call general meeting.		

4 Draft special resolution.
  4.1 Present resolution in writing to all shareholders for signature.
  or:
  4.2 Draft notice of meeting with waiver.
	Draft 14
	
	Draft 15	

	Refer to	Target completion date
5 Hold meeting (if necessary).		
6 Insert signed resolution in minute book (or prepare minutes of meeting).		
7 Prepare resolution for filing: 7.1 Secretary to sign. 7.2 Send to Registrar of Companies within 15 days: • special resolution; • fee: £10.00 (£100.00 for same-day registration).	Draft 18	
8 Await Certificate of Incorporation on change of name.		
9 Make change effective: 9.1 Print new stationery. 9.2 Display new name outside all offices, etc. 9.3 Notify all customers, suppliers, etc. 9.4 Send Certificate to bank for inspection and return. • Request new chequebook. 9.5 Notify auditors. 9.6 Amend stock of Memorandum and Articles.	Chapter 11	

CHECKLIST F

Draft Wordings

Draft Wording 1 – Memorandum of Association, Company Limited by Shares

COMPANIES ACT 1985
as amended by
COMPANIES ACT 1989

PRIVATE COMPANY LIMITED BY SHARES

MEMORANDUM OF ASSOCIATION
of
∗∗ Limited

1 The name of the company is ∗∗ Limited.

2 The registered office of the company will be in England.

3 The object of the company is to carry on business as a general commercial company.

4 The liability of the members is limited.

5 The share capital of the company is £ ∗∗ divided into ∗∗ shares of ∗∗ each.

We, the subscribers to this memorandum of association, wish to be formed into a company pursuant to this memorandum and we agree to take the number of shares shown against our respective names.

Names and addresses of subscribers	No. of shares to be taken
1	. . . .
2	. . . .
Total shares taken	

Witness(es) to both (all) the above signatures:

Name: . . . .

Address: . . . .

Occupation: . . . .

Note: For a company limited by guarantee, see next page. For alternative objects, see Draft Wording 3.

DRAFT WORDING 1

Draft Wording 2 – Memorandum of Association, Company Limited by Guarantee

COMPANIES ACT 1985
as amended by
COMPANIES ACT 1989
———
COMPANY LIMITED BY GUARANTEE
———
MEMORANDUM OF ASSOCIATION
of
＊＊ Limited

1 The name of the company is ＊＊ Limited.

2 The registered office of the company will be in England.

3 The company's object is to undertake the office of trustee of ＊＊ pension fund or any other fund or scheme set up to provide retirement benefits as defined by legislation for the time being in force and to do all such things as are incidental or conducive to that object.

4 The liability of the members is limited.

5 Every member of the company undertakes to contribute such amount as may be required (not exceeding £100) to the company's assets if it should be wound up while he/she is a member or within one year after he/she ceases to be a member, for payment of the company's debts and liabilities contracted before he/she ceases to be a member, and of the costs, charges and expenses of winding up, and for the adjustment of the rights of the contributories among themselves.

We, the subscribers to this memorandum of association, wish to be formed into a company pursuant to this memorandum.

Names and addresses of subscribers
1 ....
....
....
2 ....
....
....

Witness(es) to both (all) the above signatures:

Name: ....

Address: ....

Occupation: ....

Note: For a company limited by shares, see previous page. For alternative objects, see Draft Wording 3.

Draft Wording 3 – Alternative Objects Clauses

3 The company's object is to carry on business as a general commercial company.

3 The company's object is the carriage of passengers and goods between such places as the directors may from time to time determine and to do all such things as are incidental or conducive to that object.

3 The company's object is the carrying on of a school for boys and girls in Dundee and to do all such things as are incidental or conducive to that object.

3 The company's object is the working of certain patented inventions relating to the application of microchip technology to the improvement of food processing and to do all such things as are incidental or conducive to that object.

3 The company's object is the manufacture and development of such electronic equipment, instruments and appliances as the directors may from time to time determine and to do all such things as are incidental or conducive to that object.

3 The company's object is the publication of books, papers and periodicals of every description, to deal in books, papers and periodicals produced by others and to do all such things as are incidental or conducive to that object.

3 The company's object is to carry on the business of an investment company and for that purpose to subscribe, invest in or underwrite new issues of shares, bonds, loans or other securities, to lend money (with or without security) and from time to time to buy, sell or vary any such investments and to do all such things as are incidental or conducive to that object.

3 The company's object is to undertake the office of trustee of the ** pension fund or any other fund or scheme set up to provide retirement benefits as defined by legislation for the time being in force and to do all such things as are incidental or conducive to that object.

3 The company's object is to do all such things as are customarily done by [an investment adviser *or* a Chartered Secretary in public practice, *etc.*], to do all such things as the members [*or* 'as the directors of the company'] for the time being could do if, being duly qualified as **, they were in professional public practice on their own account, and to do all such things as are incidental or conducive to that object.

Draft Wording 4 – Articles of Association: Table A

COMPANIES (TABLES A–F) REGULATIONS 1985

TABLE A: Regulations for Management of a Company Limited by Shares

Interpretation

1   In these regulations:

'the Act' means the Companies Act 1985 including any statutory modification or re-enactment thereof for the time being in force.

'the articles' means the articles of the company.

'clear days' in relation to the period of a notice means that period excluding the day when the notice is given or deemed to be given and the day for which it is given or on which it is to take effect.

'executed' includes any mode of execution.

'office' means the registered office of the company.

'the holder' in relation to shares means the member whose name is entered in the register of members as the holder of the shares.

'the seal' means the common seal of the company.

'secretary' means the secretary of the company or any other person appointed to perform the duties of the secretary of the company, including a joint, assistant or deputy secretary.

'the United Kingdom' means Great Britain and Northern Ireland.

Unless the context otherwise requires, words or expressions contained in these regulations bear the same meaning as in the Act but excluding any statutory modification thereof not in force when these regulations become binding on the company.

Share capital

2   Subject to the provisions of the Act and without prejudice to any rights attached to any existing shares, any share may be issued with such rights or restrictions as the company may by ordinary resolution determine.

3   Subject to the provisions of the Act, shares may be issued which are to be redeemed or are to be liable to be redeemed at the option of the company or the holder on such terms and in such manner as may be provided by the articles.

4   The company may exercise the powers of paying commissions conferred by the Act. Subject to the provisions of the Act, any such commission may be satisfied by the payment of cash or by the allotment of fully or partly paid shares or partly in one way and partly in the other.

5   Except as required by law, no person shall be recognised by the company as holding any share upon any trust and (except as otherwise provided

by the articles or by law) the company shall not be bound by or recognise any interest in any share except an absolute right to the entirety thereof in the holder.

Share certificates

6   Every member, upon becoming the holder of any shares, shall be entitled without payment to one certificate for all the shares of each class held by him (and, upon transferring a part of his holding of shares of any class, to a certificate for the balance of such holding) or several certificates each for one or more of his shares upon payment for every certificate after the first of such reasonable sum as the directors may determine. Every certificate shall be sealed with the seal and shall specify the number, class and distinguishing numbers (if any) of the shares to which it relates and the amount or respective amounts paid up thereon. The company shall not be bound to issue more than one certificate for shares held jointly by several persons and delivery of a certificate to one joint holder shall be a sufficient delivery to all of them.

7   If a share certificate is defaced, worn-out, lost or destroyed, it may be renewed on such terms (if any) as to evidence and indemnity and payment of the expenses reasonably incurred by the company in investigating evidence as the directors may determine but otherwise free of charge, and (in the case of defacement or wearing-out) on delivery up of the old certificate.

Lien

8   The company shall have a first and paramount lien on every share (not being a fully paid share) for all moneys (whether presently payable or not) payable at a fixed time or called in respect of that share. The directors may at any time declare any share to be wholly or in part exempt from the provisions of this regulation. The company's lien on a share shall extend to any amount payable in respect of it.

9   The company may sell in such manner as the directors determine any shares on which the company has a lien if a sum in respect of which the lien exists is presently payable and is not paid within fourteen clear days after notice has been given to the holder of the share or to the person entitled to it in consequence of the death or bankruptcy of the holder, demanding payment and stating that if the notice is not complied with the shares may be sold.

10 To give effect to a sale the directors may authorise some person to execute an instrument of transfer of the shares sold to, or in accordance with the directions of, the purchaser. The title of the transferee to the shares shall not be affected by any irregularity in or invalidity of the proceedings in reference to the sale.

11 The net proceeds of the sale, after payment of the costs, shall be applied in payment of so much of the sum for which the lien exists as is presently payable, and any residue shall (upon surrender to the company for cancellation of the certificate for the shares sold and subject to a like lien for any moneys not presently payable as existed upon the shares before the sale) be paid to the person entitled to the shares at the date of the sale.

Calls on shares and forfeiture

12 Subject to the terms of allotment, the directors may make calls upon the members in respect of any moneys unpaid on their shares (whether in respect of nominal value or premium) and each member shall (subject to receiving at least fourteen clear days' notice specifying when and where payment is to be made) pay to the company as required by the notice the amount called on his shares. A call may be required to be paid by instalments. A call may, before receipt by the company of any sum due thereunder, be revoked in whole or part and payment of a call may be postponed in whole or part. A person upon whom a call is made shall remain liable for calls made upon him notwithstanding the subsequent transfer of the shares in respect whereof the call was made.

13 A call shall be deemed to have been made at the time when the resolution of the directors authorising the call was passed.

14 The joint holders of a share shall be jointly and severally liable to pay all calls in respect thereof.

15 If a call remains unpaid after it has become due and payable the person from whom it is due and payable shall pay interest on the amount unpaid from the day it became due and payable until it is paid at the rate fixed by the terms of allotment of the share or in the notice of the call or, if no rate is fixed, at the appropriate rate (as defined by the Act) but the directors may waive payment of the interest wholly or in part.

16 An amount payable in respect of a share on allotment or at any fixed date, whether in respect of nominal value or premium or as an instalment of a call, shall be deemed to be a call and if it is not paid the provisions of the articles shall apply as if that amount had become due and payable by virtue of a call.

17 Subject to the terms of allotment, the directors may make arrangements on the issue of shares for a difference between the holders in the amounts and times of payment of calls on their shares.

18 If a call remains unpaid after it has become due and payable the directors may give to the person from whom it is due not less than fourteen clear days' notice requiring payment of the amount unpaid together with any interest which may have accrued. The notice shall name the place where payment is to be made and shall state that if the notice is not complied with the shares in respect of which the call was made will be liable to be forfeited.

19 If the notice is not complied with any share in respect of which it was given may, before the payment required by the notice has been made, be forfeited by a resolution of the directors and the forfeiture shall include all dividends or other moneys payable in respect of the forfeited shares and not paid before the forfeiture.

20 Subject to the provisions of the Act, a forfeited share may be sold, re-allotted or otherwise disposed of on such terms and in such manner as the directors determine either to the person who was before the forfeiture the holder or to any other person and at any time before sale, re-allotment or other disposition, the forfeiture may be cancelled on such terms as the directors think fit. Where for the purposes of its disposal a forfeited share is to be transferred to any person the directors may authorise some person to execute an instrument of transfer of the share to that person.

21 A person any of whose shares have been forfeited shall cease to be a member in respect of them and shall surrender to the company for cancellation the certificate for the shares forfeited but shall remain liable to the company for all moneys which at the date of forfeiture were presently payable by him to the company in respect of those shares with interest at the rate at which interest was payable on those moneys before the forfeiture or, if no interest was so payable, at the appropriate rate (as defined in the Act) from the date of forfeiture until payment but the directors may waive payment wholly or in part or enforce payment without any allowance for the value of the shares at the time of forfeiture or for any consideration received on their disposal.

22 A statutory declaration by a director or the secretary that a share has been forfeited on a specified date shall be conclusive evidence of the facts stated in it as against all persons claiming to be entitled to the share and the declaration shall (subject to the execution of an instrument of transfer if necessary) constitute a good title to the share and the person to whom the share is disposed of shall not be bound to see to the application of the consideration, if any, nor shall his title to the share be affected by any irregularity in or invalidity of the proceedings in reference to the forfeiture or disposal of the share.

Transfer of shares

23 The instrument of transfer of a share may be in any usual form or in any other form which the directors may approve and shall be executed by or on behalf of the transferor and, unless the share is fully paid, by or on behalf of the transferee.

24 The directors may refuse to register the transfer of a share which is not fully paid to a person of whom they do not approve and they may refuse to register the transfer of a share on which the company has a lien. They may also refuse to register a transfer unless:

(a) it is lodged at the office or at such other place as the directors may appoint and is accompanied by the certificate for the shares to which it relates and such other evidence as the directors may reasonably require to show the right of the transferor to make the transfer;

(b) it is in respect of only one class of shares; and

(c) it is in favour of not more than four transferees.

25 If the directors refuse to register a transfer of a share, they shall within two months after the date on which the transfer was lodged with the company send to the transferee notice of the refusal.

26 The registration of transfers of shares or of transfers of any class of shares may be suspended at such times and for such periods (not exceeding thirty days in any year) as the directors may determine.

27 No fee shall be charged for the registration of any instrument of transfer or other document relating to or affecting the title to any share.

28 The company shall be entitled to retain any instrument of transfer which is registered, but any instrument of transfer which the directors refuse to register shall be returned to the person lodging it when notice of the refusal is given.

Transmission of shares

29 If a member dies the survivor or survivors where he was a joint holder, and his personal representatives where he was a sole holder or the only survivor of joint holders, shall be the only persons recognised by the company as having any title to his interest; but nothing herein contained shall release the estate of a deceased member from any liability in respect of any share which had been jointly held by him.

30 A person becoming entitled to a share in consequence of the death or bankruptcy of a member may, upon such evidence being produced as the directors may properly require, elect either to become the holder of the share or to have some person nominated by him registered as the transferee. If he elects to have another person registered he shall execute an instrument of transfer of the share to that person. All the articles relating to the transfer of shares shall apply to the notice or instrument of transfer as if it were an instrument of transfer executed by the member and the death or bankruptcy of the member had not occurred.

31 A person becoming entitled to a share in consequence of the death or bankruptcy of a member shall have the rights to which he would be entitled if he were the holder of the share, except that he shall not, before being registered as the holder of the share, be entitled in respect of it to attend or vote at any meeting of the company or at any separate meeting of the holders of any class of shares in the company.

Alteration of share capital

32 The company may by ordinary resolution:
   (a) increase its share capital by new shares of such amount as the resolution prescribes;
   (b) consolidate and divide all or any of its share capital into shares of larger amount than its existing shares;
   (c) subject to the provisions of the Act, sub-divide its shares, or any of them, into shares of smaller amount and the resolution may determine that, as between the shares resulting from the sub-division, any of them may have any preference or advantage as compared with the others; and
   (d) cancel shares which, at the date of the passing of the resolution, have not been taken or agreed to be taken by any person and diminish the amount of its share capital by the amount of the shares so cancelled.

33 Whenever as a result of a consolidation of shares any members would become entitled to fractions of a share, the directors may, on behalf of those members, sell the shares representing the fractions for the best price reasonably obtainable to any person (including, subject to the provisions of the Act, the company) and distribute the net proceeds of sale in due proportion among those members, and the directors may authorise some person to execute an instrument of transfer of the shares to, or in accordance with the directions of, the purchaser. The transferee shall not be bound to see to the application of the purchase money nor shall his title to the shares be affected by any irregularity in or invalidity of the proceedings in reference to the sale.

34 Subject to the provisions of the Act, the company may by special resolution reduce its share capital, any capital redemption reserve and any share premium account in any way.

Purchase of own shares

35 Subject to the provisions of the Act, the company may purchase its own shares (including any redeemable shares) and, if it is a private company, make a payment in respect of the redemption or purchase of its own shares otherwise than out of distributable profits of the company or the proceeds of a fresh issue of shares.

General meetings

36 All general meetings other than annual general meetings shall be called extraordinary general meetings.

DRAFT WORDING 4

37 The directors may call general meetings and, on the requisition of members pursuant to the provisions of the Act, shall forthwith proceed to convene an extraordinary general meeting for a date not later than eight weeks after receipt of the requisition. If there are not within the United Kingdom sufficient directors to call a general meeting, any director or any member of the company may call a general meeting.

Notice of general meetings

38 An annual general meeting and an extraordinary general meeting called for the passing of a special resolution or a resolution appointing a person as a director shall be called by at least twenty-one clear days' notice. All other extraordinary general meetings shall be called by at least fourteen clear days' notice but a general meeting may be called by shorter notice if it is so agreed:

(a) in the case of an annual general meeting, by all the members entitled to attend and vote thereat; and

(b) in the case of any other meeting by a majority in number of the members having a right to attend and vote being a majority together holding not less than ninety-five per cent in nominal value of the shares giving that right.

The notice shall specify the time and place of the meeting and the general nature of the business to be transacted and, in the case of an annual general meeting, shall specify the meeting as such.

Subject to the provisions of the articles and to any restrictions imposed on any shares, the notice shall be given to all the members, to all persons entitled to a share in consequence of the death or bankruptcy of a member and to the directors and auditors.

39 The accidental omission to give notice of a meeting to, or the non-receipt of notice of a meeting by, any person entitled to receive notice shall not invalidate the proceedings at that meeting.

Proceedings at general meetings

40 No business shall be transacted at any meeting unless a quorum is present. Two persons entitled to vote upon the business to be transacted, each being a member or a proxy for a member or a duly authorised representative of a corporation, shall be a quorum.

41 If such a quorum is not present within half an hour from the time appointed for the meeting, or if during a meeting such a quorum ceases to be present, the meeting shall stand adjourned to the same day in the next week at the same time and place or to such time and place as the directors may determine.

42 The chairman, if any, of the board of directors or in his absence some other director nominated by the directors shall preside as chairman of the meeting, but if neither the chairman nor such other director (if any) be present within fifteen minutes after the time appointed for holding the meeting and willing to act, the directors present shall elect one of their number to be chairman and, if there is only one director present and willing to act, he shall be chairman.

43 If no director is willing to act as chairman, or if no director is present within fifteen minutes after the time appointed for holding the meeting, the members present and entitled to vote shall choose one of their number to be chairman.

44 A director shall, notwithstanding that he is not a member, be entitled to attend and speak at any general meeting and at any separate meeting of the holders of any class of shares in the company.

45 The chairman may, with the consent of a meeting at which a quorum is present (and shall if so directed by the meeting), adjourn the meeting from time to time and from place to place, but no business shall be transacted at an adjourned meeting other than business which might properly have been transacted at the meeting had the adjournment not taken place. When a meeting is adjourned for fourteen days or more, at least seven clear days' notice shall be given specifying the time and place of the adjourned meeting and the general nature of the business to be transacted. Otherwise it shall not be necessary to give any such notice.

46 A resolution put to the vote of a meeting shall be decided on a show of hands unless before, or on the declaration of the result of the show of hands a poll is duly demanded. Subject to the provisions of the Act, a poll may be demanded:
(a) by the chairman; or
(b) by at least two members having the right to vote at the meeting; or
(c) by a member or members representing not less than one-tenth of the total voting rights of all the members having the right to vote at the meeting; or
(d) by a member or members holding shares conferring a right to vote at the meeting being shares on which an aggregate sum has been paid up equal to not less than one-tenth of the total sum paid up on all the shares conferring that right;
and a demand by a person as proxy for a member shall be the same as a demand by the member.

47 Unless a poll is duly demanded a declaration by the chairman that a resolution has been carried or carried unanimously, or by a particular majority, or lost, or not carried by a particular majority and an entry to that effect in the minutes of the meeting shall be conclusive evidence of the fact without proof of the number or proportion of the votes recorded in favour of or against the resolution.

DRAFT WORDING 4

48 The demand for a poll may, before the poll is taken, be withdrawn but only with the consent of the chairman and a demand so withdrawn shall not be taken to have invalidated the result of a show of hands declared before the demand was made.

49 A poll shall be taken as the chairman directs and he may appoint scrutineers (who need not be members) and fix a time and place for declaring the result of the poll. The result of the poll shall be deemed to be the resolution of the meeting at which the poll was demanded.

50 In the case of an equality of votes, whether on a show of hands or on a poll, the chairman shall be entitled to a casting vote in addition to any other vote he may have.

51 A poll demanded on the election of a chairman or on a question of adjournment shall be taken forthwith. A poll demanded on any other question shall be taken either forthwith or at such time and place as the chairman directs not being more than thirty days after the poll is demanded. The demand for a poll shall not prevent the continuance of a meeting for the transaction of any business other than the question on which the poll was demanded. If a poll is demanded before the declaration of the result of a show of hands and the demand is duly withdrawn, the meeting shall continue as if the demand had not been made.

52 No notice need be given of a poll not taken forthwith if the time and place at which it is to be taken are announced at the meeting at which it is demanded. In any other case at least seven clear days' notice shall be given specifying the time and place at which the poll is to be taken.

53 A resolution in writing executed by or on behalf of each member who would have been entitled to vote upon it if it had been proposed at a general meeting at which he was present shall be as effectual as if it had been passed at a general meeting duly convened and held and may consist of several instruments in the like form each executed by or on behalf of one or more members.

Votes of members

54 Subject to any rights or restrictions attached to any shares, on a show of hands every member who (being an individual) is present in person or (being a corporation) is present by a duly authorised representative, not being himself a member entitled to vote, shall have one vote and on a poll every member shall have one vote for every share of which he is the holder.

55 In the case of joint holders the vote of the senior who tenders a vote, whether in person or by proxy, shall be accepted to the exclusion of the votes of the other joint holders; and seniority shall be determined by the order in which the names of the holders stand in the register of members.

56 A member in respect of whom an order has been made by any court having jurisdiction (whether in the United Kingdom or elsewhere) in matters concerning mental disorder may vote, whether on a show of hands or on a poll, by his receiver, *curator bonis* or other person authorised in that behalf appointed by that court, and any such receiver, *curator bonis* or other person may, on a poll, vote by proxy. Evidence to the satisfaction of the directors of the authority of the person claiming to exercise the right to vote shall be deposited at the office, or at such other place as is specified in accordance with the articles for the deposit of instruments of proxy, not less than 48 hours before the time appointed for holding the meeting or adjourned meeting at which the right to vote is to be exercised and in default the right to vote shall not be exercisable.

57 No member shall vote at any general meeting or at any separate meeting of the holders of any class of shares in the company, either in person or by proxy, in respect of any share held by him unless all moneys presently payable by him in respect of that share have been paid.

58 No objection shall be raised to the qualification of any voter except at the meeting or adjourned meeting at which the vote objected to is tendered, and every vote not disallowed at the meeting shall be valid. Any objection made in due time shall be referred to the chairman whose decision shall be final and conclusive.

59 On a poll votes may be given either personally or by proxy. A member may appoint more than one proxy to attend on the same occasion.

60 An instrument appointing a proxy shall be in writing, executed by or on behalf of the appointor and shall be in the following form (or in a form as near thereto as circumstances allow or in any other form which is usual or which the directors may approve):

"_____ PLC/Limited

I/We, _____ , of _____

being a member/members of the above-named company, hereby

appoint _____ of _____ ,

or failing him _____ of _____ , as my/

our proxy to vote in my/our name[s] and on my/our behalf at the

annual/extraordinary general meeting of the company, to be held on

_____ 19 ____ , and at any adjournment thereof.

Signed on _____ 19____ ."

61 Where it is desired to afford members an opportunity of instructing the proxy how he shall act the instrument appointing a proxy shall be in the following form (or in a form as near thereto as circumstances allow or in any other form which is usual or which the directors may approve):

"_____ PLC/Limited

I/We, _____ , of _____

being a member/members of the above-named company, hereby

appoint _____ of _____ ,

or failing him _____ of _____ , as my/

our proxy to vote in my/our name[s] and on my/our behalf at the

annual/extraordinary general meeting of the company, to be held on

_____ 19 ____ , and at any adjournment thereof.

This form is to be used in respect of the resolutions mentioned below as follows:

    Resolution No. 1 *for *against
    Resolution No. 2 *for *against.

*Strike out whichever is not desired.

Unless otherwise instructed, the proxy may vote as he thinks fit or abstain from voting.

Signed this _____ day of _____ 19 ____ ."

62 The instrument appointing a proxy and any authority under which it is executed or a copy of such authority certified notarially or in some other way approved by the directors may:

  (a) be deposited at the office or at such other place within the United Kingdom as is specified in the notice convening the meeting or in any instrument of proxy sent out by the company in relation to the meeting not less than 48 hours before the time for holding the meeting or adjourned meeting at which the person named in the instrument proposes to vote; or

  (b) in the case of a poll taken more than 48 hours after it is demanded, be deposited as aforesaid after the poll has been demanded and not less than 24 hours before the time appointed for the taking of the poll; or

  (c) where the poll is not taken forthwith but is taken not more than 48 hours after it was demanded, be delivered at the meeting at which the poll was demanded to the chairman or to the secretary or to any director;

and an instrument of proxy which is not deposited or delivered in a manner so permitted shall be invalid.

63 A vote given or poll demanded by proxy or by the duly authorised representative of a corporation shall be valid notwithstanding the previous

determination of the authority of the person voting or demanding a poll unless notice of the determination was received by the company at the office or at such other place at which the instrument of proxy was duly deposited before the commencement of the meeting or adjourned meeting at which the vote is given or the poll demanded or (in the case of a poll taken otherwise than on the same day as the meeting or adjourned meeting) the time appointed for taking the poll.

64 Unless otherwise determined by ordinary resolution, the number of directors (other than alternate directors) shall not be subject to any maximum but shall be not less than two.

Alternate directors

65 Any director (other than an alternate director) may appoint any other director, or any other person approved by resolution of the directors and willing to act, to be an alternate director and may remove from office an alternate director so appointed by him.

66 An alternate director shall be entitled to receive notice of all meetings of directors and of all meetings of committees of directors of which his appointor is a member, to attend and vote at any such meeting at which the director appointing him shall personally be present, and generally to perform all the functions of his appointor as director in his absence but shall not be entitled to receive any remuneration from the company for his services as an alternate director. But it shall not be necessary to give notice of such a meeting to an alternate director who is absent from the United Kingdom.

67 An alternate director shall cease to be an alternate director if his appointor ceases to be a director; but, if a director retires by rotation or otherwise but is reappointed or deemed to have been reappointed at the meeting at which he retires, any appointment of an alternate director made by him which was in force immediately prior to his retirement shall continue after his reappointment.

68 Any appointment or removal of an alternate director shall be by notice to the company signed by the director making or revoking the appointment or in any other manner approved by the directors.

69 Save as otherwise provided in the articles, an alternate director shall be deemed for all purposes to be a director and shall alone be responsible for his own acts and defaults and he shall not be deemed to be the agent of the director appointing him.

Powers of directors

70 Subject to the provisions of the Act, the memorandum and the articles and to any directions given by special resolution, the business of the company shall be managed by the directors who may exercise all the

powers of the company. No alteration of the memorandum or articles and no such direction shall invalidate any prior act of the directors which would have been valid if that alteration had not been made or that direction had not been given. The powers given by this regulation shall not be limited by any special power given to the directors by the articles and a meeting of directors at which a quorum is present may exercise all powers exercisable by the directors.

71 The directors may, by power of attorney or otherwise, appoint any person to be the agent of the company for such purposes and on such conditions as they determine, including authority for the agent to delegate all or any of his powers.

Delegation of directors' powers

72 The directors may delegate any of their powers to any committee consisting of one or more directors. They may also delegate to any managing director or any director holding any other executive office such of their powers as they consider desirable to be exercised by him. Any such delegation may be made subject to any conditions the directors may impose, and either collaterally with or to the exclusion of their own powers and may be revoked or altered. Subject to any such conditions, the proceedings of a committee with two or more members shall be governed by the articles regulating the proceedings of directors so far as they are capable of applying.

Appointment and retirement of directors

73 At the first annual general meeting all the directors shall retire from office, and at every subsequent annual general meeting one-third of the directors who are subject to retirement by rotation or, if their number is not three or a multiple of three, the number nearest to one-third shall retire from office; but, if there is only one director who is subject to retirement by rotation, he shall retire.

74 Subject to the provisions of the Act, the directors to retire by rotation shall be those who have been longest in office since their last appointment or reappointment, but as between persons who became or were last reappointed directors on the same day those to retire shall (unless they otherwise agree among themselves) be determined by lot.

75 If the company, at the meeting at which a director retires by rotation, does not fill the vacancy the retiring director shall, if willing to act, be deemed to have been reappointed unless at the meeting it is resolved not to fill the vacancy or unless a resolution for the reappointment of the director is put to the meeting and lost.

76 No person other than a director retiring by rotation shall be appointed or reappointed a director at any general meeting unless:

(a) he is recommended by the directors; or

(b) not less than fourteen nor more than thirty-five clear days before the date appointed for the meeting, notice executed by a member qualified to vote at the meeting has been given to the company of the intention to propose that person for appointment or reappointment stating the particulars which would, if he were so appointed or reappointed, be required to be included in the company's register of directors together with notice executed by that person of his willingness to be appointed or reappointed.

77 Not less than seven nor more than twenty-eight clear days before the date appointed for holding a general meeting notice shall be given to all who are entitled to receive notice of the meeting of any person (other than a director retiring by rotation at the meeting) who is recommended by the directors for appointment or reappointment as a director at the meeting or in respect of whom notice has been duly given to the company of the intention to propose him at the meeting for appointment or reappointment as a director. The notice shall give the particulars of that person which would, if he were so appointed or reappointed, be required to be included in the company's register of directors.

78 Subject as aforesaid, the company may by ordinary resolution appoint a person who is willing to act to be a director either to fill a vacancy or as an additional director and may also determine the rotation in which any additional directors are to retire.

79 The directors may appoint a person who is willing to act to be a director, either to fill a vacancy or as an additional director, provided that the appointment does not cause the number of directors to exceed any number fixed by or in accordance with the articles as the maximum number of directors. A director so appointed shall hold office only until the next following annual general meeting and shall not be taken into account in determining the directors who are to retire by rotation at the meeting. If not reappointed at such annual general meeting, he shall vacate office at the conclusion thereof.

80 Subject as aforesaid, a director who retires at an annual general meeting may, if willing to act, be reappointed. If he is not reappointed, he shall retain office until the meeting appoints someone in his place, or if it does not do so, until the end of the meeting.

Disqualification and removal of directors

81 The office of a director shall be vacated if:

(a) he ceases to be a director by virtue of any provision of the Act or he becomes prohibited by law from being a director; or

(b) he becomes bankrupt or makes any arrangement or composition with his creditors generally; or

(c) he is, or may be, suffering from mental disorder and either:

(i) he is admitted to hospital in pursuance of an application for admission for treatment under the Mental Health Act 1983 or, in Scotland, an application for admission under the Mental Health (Scotland) Act 1960,

or

(ii) an order is made by a court having jurisdiction (whether in the United Kingdom or elsewhere) in matters concerning mental disorder for his detention or for the appointment of a receiver, *curator bonis* or other person to exercise powers with respect to his property or affairs; or

(d) he resigns his office by notice to the company; or

(e) he shall for more than six consecutive months have been absent without permission of the directors from meetings of directors held during that period and the directors resolve that his office be vacated.

Remuneration of directors

82 The directors shall be entitled to such remuneration as the company may by ordinary resolution determine and, unless the resolution provides otherwise, the remuneration shall be deemed to accrue from day to day.

Directors' expenses

83 The directors may be paid all travelling, hotel, and other expenses properly incurred by them in connection with their attendance at meetings of directors or committees of directors or general meetings or separate meetings of the holders of any class of shares or of debentures of the company or otherwise in connection with the discharge of their duties.

Directors' appointments and interests

84 Subject to the provisions of the Act, the directors may appoint one or more of their number to the office of managing director or to any other executive office under the company and may enter into an agreement or arrangement with any director for his employment by the company or for the provision by him of any services outside the scope of the ordinary duties of a director. Any such appointment, agreement or arrangement may be made upon such terms as the directors determine and they may remunerate any such director for his services as they think fit. Any appointment of a director to an executive office shall terminate if he ceases to be a director but without prejudice to any claim to damages for breach of the contract of service between the director and the company. A managing director and a director holding any other executive office shall not be subject to retirement by rotation.

85 Subject to the provisions of the Act, and provided that he has disclosed
to the directors the nature and extent of any material interest of his, a
director notwithstanding his office:

(a) may be a party to, or otherwise interested in, any transaction or
arrangement with the company or in which the company is otherwise interested;

(b) may be a director or other officer of, or employed by, or a party to
any transaction or arrangement with, or otherwise interested in, any
body corporate promoted by the company or in which the company
is otherwise interested; and

(c) shall not, by reason of his office, be accountable to the company for
any benefit which he derives from any such office or employment or
from any such transaction or arrangement or from any interest in
any such body corporate and no such transaction or arrangement
shall be liable to be avoided on the ground of any such interest or
benefit.

86 For the purposes of regulation 85:

(a) a general notice given to the directors that a director is to be regarded
as having an interest of the nature and extent specified in the notice
in any transaction or arrangement in which a specified person or
class of persons is interested shall be deemed to be a disclosure that
the director has an interest in any such transaction of the nature and
extent so specified; and

(b) an interest of which a director has no knowledge and of which it is
unreasonable to expect him to have knowledge shall not be treated
as an interest of his.

Directors' gratuities and pensions

87 The directors may provide benefits, whether by the payment of gratu-
ities or pensions or by insurance or otherwise, for any director who has
held but no longer holds any executive office or employment with the
company or with any body corporate which is or has been a subsidiary
of the company or a predecessor in business of the company or of any
such subsidiary, and for any member of his family (including a spouse
and a former spouse) or any person who is or was dependent on him,
and may (as well before as after he ceases to hold such office or employment) contribute to any fund and pay premiums for the purchase or
provision of any such benefit.

Proceedings of directors

88 Subject to the provisions of the articles, the directors may regulate their
proceedings as they think fit. A director may, and the secretary at the
request of a director shall, call a meeting of the directors. It shall not be

necessary to give notice of a meeting to a director who is absent from the United Kingdom. Questions arising at a meeting shall be decided by a majority of votes. In the case of an equality of votes, the chairman shall have a second or casting vote. A director who is also an alternate director shall be entitled in the absence of his appointor to a separate vote on behalf of his appointor in addition to his own vote.

89 The quorum for the transaction of the business of the directors may be fixed by the directors and unless so fixed at any other number shall be two. A person who holds office only as an alternate director shall, if his appointor is not present, be counted in the quorum.

90 The continuing directors or a sole continuing director may act notwithstanding any vacancies in their number, but, if the number of directors is less than the number fixed as the quorum, the continuing directors or director may act only for the purpose of filling vacancies or of calling a general meeting.

91 The directors may appoint one of their number to be the chairman of the board of directors and may at any time remove him from that office. Unless he is unwilling to do so, the director so appointed shall preside at every meeting of directors at which he is present. But if there is no director holding that office, or if the director holding it is unwilling to preside or is not present within five minutes, after the time appointed for the meeting, the directors present may appoint one of their number to be chairman of the meeting.

92 All acts done by a meeting of directors, or of a committee of directors, or by a person acting as a director shall, notwithstanding that it be afterwards discovered that there was a defect in the appointment of any director or that any of them were disqualified from holding office, or had vacated office, or were not entitled to vote, be as valid as if every such person had been duly appointed and was qualified and had continued to be a director and had been entitled to vote.

93 A resolution in writing signed by all the directors entitled to receive notice of a meeting of directors or of a committee of directors shall be as valid and effectual as if it had been passed at a meeting of directors or (as the case may be) a committee of directors duly convened and held and may consist of several documents in the like form each signed by one or more directors; but a resolution signed by an alternate director need not also be signed by his appointor and, if it is signed by a director who has appointed an alternate director, it need not be signed by the alternate director in that capacity.

94 Save as otherwise provided by the articles, a director shall not vote at a meeting of directors or of a committee of directors on any resolution concerning a matter in which he has, directly or indirectly, an interest or duty which is material and which conflicts or may conflict with the

interests of the company unless his interest or duty arises only because the case falls within one or more of the following paragraphs:

(a) the resolution relates to the giving to him of a guarantee, security, or indemnity in respect of money lent to, or an obligation incurred by him for the benefit of, the company or any of its subsidiaries;

(b) the resolution relates to the giving to a third party of a guarantee, security, or indemnity in respect of an obligation of the company or any of its subsidiaries for which the director has assumed responsibility in whole or part and whether alone or jointly with others under a guarantee of indemnity or by the giving of security;

(c) his interest arises by virtue of his subscribing or agreeing to subscribe for any shares, debentures or other securities of the company or any of its subsidiaries, or by virtue of his being, or intending to become, a participant in the underwriting or sub-underwriting of an offer of any such shares, debentures, or other securities by the company or any of its subsidiaries for subscription, purchase or exchange;

(d) the resolution relates in any way to a retirement benefits scheme which has been approved, or is conditional upon approval, by the board of Inland Revenue for taxation purposes.

For the purposes of this regulation, an interest of a person who is, for any purpose of the Act (excluding any statutory modification thereof not in force when this regulation becomes binding on the company), connected with a director shall be treated as an interest of the director and, in relation to an alternate director, an interest of his appointor shall be treated as an interest of the alternate director without prejudice to any interest which the alternate director has otherwise.

95 A director shall not be counted in the quorum present at a meeting in relation to a resolution on which he is not entitled to vote.

96 The company may by ordinary resolution suspend or relax to any extent, either generally or in respect of any particular matter, any provision of the articles prohibiting a director from voting at a meeting of directors or of a committee of directors.

97 Where proposals are under consideration concerning the appointment of two or more directors to offices or employments with the company or any body corporate in which the company is interested the proposals may be divided and considered in relation to each director separately and (provided he is not for another reason precluded from voting) each of the directors concerned shall be entitled to vote and be counted in the quorum in respect of each resolution except that concerning his own appointment.

98 If a question arises at a meeting of directors or of a committee of directors as to the right of a director to vote, the question may, before the conclusion of the meeting, be referred to the chairman of the meeting

and his ruling in relation to any director other than himself shall be final and conclusive.

Secretary

99 Subject to the provisions of the Act, the secretary shall be appointed by the directors for such term, at such remuneration and upon such conditions as they may think fit; and any secretary so appointed may be removed by them.

Minutes

100 The directors shall cause minutes to be made in books kept for the purpose:
(a) of all appointments of officers made by the directors; and
(b) of all proceedings at meetings of the company, of the holders of any class of shares in the company, and of the directors, and of committees of directors, including the names of the directors present at each such meeting.

The seal

101 The seal shall only be used by the authority of the directors or of a committee of directors authorised by the directors. The directors may determine who shall sign any instrument to which the seal is affixed and unless otherwise so determined it shall be signed by a director and by the secretary or by a second director.

Dividends

102 Subject to the provisions of the Act, the company may by ordinary resolution declare dividends in accordance with the respective rights of the members, but no dividend shall exceed the amount recommended by the directors.

103 Subject to the provisions of the Act, the directors may pay interim dividends if it appears to them that they are justified by the profits of the company available for distribution. If the share capital is divided into different classes, the directors may pay interim dividends on shares which confer deferred or non-preferred rights with regard to dividend as well as on shares which confer preferential rights with regard to dividend, but no interim dividend shall be paid on shares carrying deferred or non-preferred rights if at the time of payment, any preferential dividend is in arrear. The directors may also pay at intervals settled by them any dividend payable at a fixed rate if it appears to them that the profits available for distribution justify the payment. Provided the directors act in good faith they shall not incur any liability to the holders of shares conferring preferred rights for any loss they may suffer by the lawful payment of an interim dividend on any shares having deferred or non-preferred rights.

104 Except as otherwise provided by the rights attached to shares, all dividends shall be declared and paid according to the amounts paid up on the shares on which the dividend is paid. All dividends shall be apportioned and paid proportionately to the amounts paid up on the shares during any portion or portions of the period in respect of which the dividend is paid; but, if any share is issued on terms providing that it shall rank for dividend as from a particular date, that share shall rank for dividend accordingly.

105 A general meeting declaring a dividend may, upon the recommendation of the directors, direct that it shall be satisfied wholly or partly by the distribution of assets and, where any difficulty arises in regard to the distribution, the directors may settle the same and in particular may issue fractional certificates and fix the value for distribution of any assets and may determine that cash shall be paid to any member upon the footing of the value so fixed in order to adjust the rights of members and may vest any assets in trustees.

106 Any dividend or other moneys payable in respect of a share may be paid by cheque sent by post to the registered address of the person entitled or, if two or more persons are the holders of the share or are jointly entitled to it by reason of the death or bankruptcy of the holder, to the registered address of that one of those persons who is first named in the register of members or to such person and to such address as the person or persons entitled may in writing direct. Every cheque shall be made payable to the order of the persons entitled or to such other person as the person or persons entitled may in writing direct and payment of the cheque shall be a good discharge to the company. Any joint holder or other person jointly entitled to a share as aforesaid may give receipts for any dividend or other moneys payable in respect of the share.

107 No dividend or other moneys payable in respect of a share shall bear interest against the company unless otherwise provided by the rights attached to the share.

108 Any dividend which has remained unclaimed for twelve years from the date when it became due for payment shall, if the directors so resolve, be forfeited and cease to remain owing by the company.

Accounts

109 No member shall (as such) have any right of inspecting any accounting records or other book or document of the company except as conferred by statute or authorised by the directors or by ordinary resolution of the company.

Capitalisation of profits

110 The directors may with the authority of an ordinary resolution of the company:

(a) subject as hereinafter provided, resolve to capitalise any undivided profits of the company not required for paying any preferential dividend (whether or not they are available for distribution) or any sum standing to the credit of the company's share premium account or capital redemption reserve;

(b) appropriate the sum resolved to be capitalised to the members who would have been entitled to it if it were distributed by way of dividend and in the same proportions and apply such sum on their behalf either in or towards paying up the amounts, if any, for the time being unpaid on any shares held by them respectively, or in paying up in full unissued shares or debentures of the company of a nominal amount equal to that sum, and allot the shares or debentures credited as fully paid to those members, or as they may direct, in those proportions, or partly in one way and partly in the other; but the share premium account, the capital redemption reserve, and any profits which are not available for distribution may, for the purposes of this regulation, only be applied in paying up unissued shares to be allotted to members credited as fully paid;

(c) make such provision by the issue of fractional certificates or by payment in cash or otherwise as they determine in the case of shares or debentures becoming distributable under this regulation in fractions; and

(d) authorise any person to enter on behalf of all the members concerned into an agreement with the company providing for the allotment to them respectively, credited as fully paid, of any shares or debentures to which they are entitled upon such capitalisation, any agreement made under such authority being binding on all such members.

Notices

111 Any notice to be given to or by any person pursuant to the articles shall be in writing except that a notice calling a meeting of the directors need not be in writing.

112 The company may give any notice to a member either personally or by sending it by post in a prepaid envelope addressed to the member at his registered address or by leaving it at that address. In the case of joint holders of a share, all notices shall be given to the joint holder whose name stands first in the register of members in respect of the joint holding and notice so given shall be sufficient notice to all the joint holders. A member whose registered address is not within the

United Kingdom and who gives to the company an address within the United Kingdom at which notices may be given to him shall be entitled to have notices given to him at the address, but otherwise no such member shall be entitled to receive any notice from the company.

113 A member present, either in person or by proxy, at any meeting of the company or of the holders of any class of shares in the company shall be deemed to have received notice of the meeting and, where requisite, of the purposes for which it was called.

114 Every person who becomes entitled to a share shall be bound by any notice in respect of that share which, before his name is entered in the register of members, has been duly given to a person from whom he derives his title.

115 Proof that an envelope containing a notice was properly addressed, prepaid and posted shall be conclusive evidence that the notice was given. A notice shall, unless the contrary is proved, be deemed to be given at the expiration of 48 hours after the envelope containing it was posted.

116 A notice may be given by the company to the persons entitled to a share in consequence of the death or bankruptcy of a member by sending or delivering it, in any manner authorised by the articles for the giving of notice to a member, addressed to them by name, or by the title of representatives of the deceased, or trustee of the bankrupt or by any like description at the address, if any, within the United Kingdom supplied for that purpose by the persons claiming to be so entitled. Until such an address has been supplied, a notice may be given in any manner in which it might have been given if the death or bankruptcy had not occurred.

Winding up

117 If the company is wound up, the liquidator may, with the sanction of an extraordinary resolution of the company and any other sanction required by the Act, divide among the members *in specie* the whole or any part of the assets of the company and may, for that purpose, value any assets and determine how the division shall be carried out as between the members or different classes of members. The liquidator may, with the like sanction, vest the whole or any part of the assets in trustees upon such trusts for the benefit of the members as he with the like sanction determines, but no member shall be compelled to accept any assets upon which there is a liability.

Indemnity

118 Subject to the provisions of the Act but without prejudice to any indemnity to which a director may otherwise be entitled, every

director or other officer or auditor of the company shall be indemnified out of the assets of the company against any liability incurred by him in defending any proceedings, whether civil or criminal, in which judgment is given in his favour or in which he is acquitted or in connection with any application in which relief is granted to him by the court from liability for negligence, default, breach of duty or breach of trust in relation to the affairs of the company.

DRAFT WORDING 4

Draft Wording 5 – Short-Form Articles

COMPANIES ACT 1985

COMPANIES ACT 1989
———
COMPANY LIMITED BY SHARES
———
ARTICLES OF ASSOCIATION

of

** Limited
———

Preliminary

1   The regulations in Table A in the schedule to the Companies (Tables A to F) Regulations 1985, as amended, shall apply to this company except as hereinafter provided or where inconsistent with the following regulations.

2   Regulations ** and ** of Table A shall not apply.

Share capital

3   The share capital of the company comprises ** shares of £ ** each which rank *pari passu* in all respects.

3A The share capital of the company comprises ** preference shares and ** ordinary shares, all of £ ** each.

[*Set out here the special rights of each class of shares, as given in the terms of issue.*]

4   No offer shall be made to the public of any shares or other securities of the company.

5   The directors may at their absolute discretion, without giving any reason, decline to register any transfer of shares, and accordingly regulation 24 of Table A shall not apply.

6   The company shall not issue any shares otherwise than fully paid on allotment.

7   The directors may, pursuant to section 80 of the Act, at any time within five years from the date of incorporation of the company, allot any part of the share capital in the company for the time being authorised but un-issued.

8   Sections 89(1) and 90(1) to (6) of the Act shall not apply to the company and accordingly the directors may allot and issue shares otherwise than in proportion to existing holdings.

Seal

9   The company shall not have a common seal and accordingly regulation 101 of Table A shall not apply to the company and regulation 6 shall apply as if the words 'shall be sealed with the seal' were deleted and replaced by 'signed by any one director and by the secretary'.

General meetings

10 If and so long as the company has only one member:

(a) that member, or a proxy for that member, or if that member is a corporation then a duly appointed representative of that member shall be a quorum at any meeting.

(b) a resolution in writing signed by that member shall be as effective for all purposes as if passed by a unanimous vote at a general meeting of the company.

11 If the company has at the time of a general meeting more than one shareholder, then no business shall be transacted at that meeting unless two persons entitled to vote upon the business to be transacted are present, each being a member or a proxy for a member or a duly authorised representative of a corporation which is a member

[*optional addition*] ... provided such member or members together hold a majority [or not less than ∗∗ %] of the issued share capital.

[*alternative*] ... provided Mr John Smith, while he holds not less than ∗∗ % of the issued share capital, is one of those members.

11 Regulation 54 of Table A shall apply subject to the proviso that on a poll for a special resolution [*and/or:* 'a resolution to increase the share capital'] no member shall cast more than ∗∗ votes.

[*or:* 'cast any votes in respect of shares in excess of ∗∗ % of the shares entitled to vote'].

Directors

12 Unless otherwise determined by ordinary resolution, the number of directors (other than alternate directors) shall not be less than ∗∗ nor more than ∗∗ .

or shall not be less than ∗∗ but shall not be subject to any maximum.

13 Directors shall not be required to retire by rotation and accordingly regulations 73, 74 and 75 of Table A shall not apply.

13 The directors shall have power at any time, and from time to time, to appoint any person to be a director, but so that the total number of directors shall not exceed the limit fixed by the preceding regulation. Regulations 73 to 80 of Table A shall not apply.

13 A member or members holding a majority of the issued [ordinary?] shares shall have power from time to time and at any time, by instrument in writing signed by the member or members (or if a company, signed by its secretary) to appoint any person as a director or to remove from office any director howsoever appointed.

13 So long as ∗∗ Limited remains a member of the company

[*or*] So long as ∗∗ Limited holds not less than ∗∗ % of the issued share capital of the company

it shall be entitled to appoint ∗∗ directors.

[*Repeat as often as desired, for other major shareholders*].

Either/Any of these members may at any time and without giving any reason remove any director it has appointed and may appoint a new director to fill any vacancy among the directors it has appointed whether arising from removal or for any other reason. No director of the company shall be appointed except under this regulation.

14   The quorum necessary for the transaction of the business of the directors shall be two directors of whom one shall be a director nominated by ✳✳ Limited and one shall be a director nominated by ✳✳ Limited.

15   Regulation 88 of Table A shall apply with the exception of the sentence commencing: 'Questions arising ...' for which the following shall be substituted: 'Questions arising at any meeting of the directors shall be decided by a majority of votes but so that all the directors appointed by ✳✳ Limited shall together have one vote and all the directors appointed by ✳✳ Limited shall together have one vote, but without prejudice to the chairman's casting vote.'

16   No person shall be disqualified from being or becoming a director by reason only of having attained the age of 70 years.

16   Section 293 of the Act shall apply to the company but as if the age of ✳✳ years were substituted for the age of 70 years.

Borrowing powers

17   Regulation 70 of Table A shall apply but subject to the proviso that if the directors exercise the powers of the company to borrow money then the amount for the time being remaining undischarged of moneys borrowed shall not at any time, without the previous sanction of an ordinary resolution, exceed the sum of £ ✳✳ , but no lender or other person dealing with the company shall be concerned to see or enquire whether this limit is observed.

Names and addresses of subscribers
1 ....
....
2 ....
....

Witness(es) to both (all) the above signatures:

Name: ....

Address: ....

Occupation: ....

Note: This document is not intended to be adopted in its entirety. Some regulations are alternatives. In particular, where two regulations have been given the same number, only one of these alternatives should be included. After deleting what is not required, the remaining regulations should be renumbered consecutively.

Draft Wording 6 – Board Meeting: Notice and Agenda

∗∗ Limited

[ADDRESS]
[DATE]

To the Directors,
∗∗ Limited

NOTICE OF BOARD MEETING

You are invited to the first meeting of the directors of ∗∗ Limited to be held at [PLACE] on [DATE] at [TIME] for the following business:

1   To report the incorporation of the company, noting the names of the persons appointed as first directors and as secretary of the company.

2   To elect a chairman.

3   To appoint additional directors.

4   To note the appointment of [an] alternate director[s].

5   To appoint and approve the terms of employment of a chief executive.

6   To open an account at ∗∗ Bank plc.

7   To (allot shares and) sign share certificates.

8   To appoint auditors.

9   To decide the accounting reference date.

10   To receive directors' declarations of interest.

I enclose a copy of the Memorandum and Articles of Association and, in reference to item 10, some explanatory notes and a form which you may care to complete and bring to the meeting.

Yours sincerely,

. . . .

Company secretary

Draft Wording 7 – Draft Minutes

** Limited

MINUTES
of the first meeting of the Board of Directors
held at [PLACE] on [DATE] commencing at [TIME].

Present: Mr ————————————— (Chairman)
Mrs ——————————
Ms ——————————
Mr ——————————

In attendance: Ms ————————————— (Secretary)

1 Incorporation

The Secretary laid upon the table:

- The Certificate of Incorporation dated [DATE].
- Copies of the Memorandum and Articles of Association.
- A copy of form 10 as filed with the Registrar of Companies from which it was noted that the following had been appointed the first directors of the company:

Mr ——————————
Mrs ——————————
Ms ——————————
Mr ——————————

that Ms ————————— had been appointed Secretary of the company and that the registered office of the company was at [ADDRESS].

2 Chairman

It was resolved that Mr ————————————— be and is hereby appointed Chairman of the board of directors.

3 Additional directors

It was resolved that Mr [NAME IN FULL] be and is hereby appointed an additional director of the company.

4 Alternate director

Mr [DIRECTOR], a director of the company, laid before the meeting a letter by which he appointed Mr [ALTERNATE'S NAME IN FULL] his alternate to attend, vote and generally to perform all the functions of a director in the absence of Mr [DIRECTOR].

5 Chief Executive Officer

It was resolved that Mr [NAME IN FULL] be appointed Chief Executive Officer of the company on the terms and with the powers set out in a letter of appointment produced to the meeting. This letter, on acceptance by Mr _____, would constitute his formal contract of employment. After discussion, the terms were agreed. Mr [CHAIRMAN] signed the letter in duplicate on behalf of the company and handed both copies to Mr [CHIEF EXECUTIVE] who signed his acceptance on both copies, retaining one and handing the other to the company secretary for safe keeping.

6 Bank account

It was resolved that an account be opened with _____ Bank plc and that ... [*continue with wording of resolution from the bank's printed form, taking particular care when inserting names of cheque signatories*].

7 Share capital

It was noted that the share capital of the company was £___ divided into [NUMBER] shares of £ [NOMINAL VALUE] each and that the capital had been fully subscribed by the subscribers to the Memorandum of Association. A cheque (Cheques) representing the subscription money was (were) laid upon the table and it was resolved:

7.1 that the shares, being fully paid, henceforth bear no distinguishing numbers and

7.2 that share certificates be executed by the company with the signatures of Mr [ONE OF THE DIRECTORS] and of the Secretary as follows:

[FIRST SHAREHOLDER] [NUMBER] shares, fully paid

[SECOND SHAREHOLDER] [NUMBER] shares, fully paid

8 Loan to parent company

It was resolved that the sum of £___ be loaned to [NAME OF PARENT] plc, free of interest, subject to recall at any time on 24 hours' notice.

9 Auditors and accounts

It was resolved:

9.1 that _____ , Chartered Accountants, be and are hereby appointed auditors of the company;

9.2 that the accounting reference date of the company be [DATE, OMITTING YEAR] and that the first accounts of the company be made up to [DATE, INCLUDING YEAR].

10 Directors' declarations of interests.

Mr _____ , a director of the company, gave written notice that he was a member of and therefore had a pecuniary interest in any contract made with any of the following companies:

_____ Limited

_____ Limited

_____ Limited

Ms _____ , also a director, gave similar notice is respect of:

_____ Limited

11 Regular board meetings

It was agreed that board meetings be held at the registered office of the company at [TIME] on the [FIRST WEDNESDAY] of each month.

That concluded the business of the meeting.

Draft Wording 8 – Share Certificate

∗∗ Limited

Incorporated under Companies Act 1985 as amended by
Companies Act 1989

SHARE CERTIFICATE

This is to certify that [NAME OF SHAREHOLDER] is the registered holder
of [NUMBER] [ORDINARY, PREFERENCE, *etc.*] shares in the capital of
_____ Limited subject to the Memorandum and Articles
of Association.

Executed by the Company:

....
Director

....
Secretary

Draft Wording 9 – Register of Members

Name:

Address:

Became a shareholder on:

Shares held:

Membership ceased:

Name:

Address:

Became a shareholder on:

Shares held:

Membership ceased:

Name:

Address:

Became a shareholder on:

Shares held:

Membership ceased:

Name:

Address:

Became a shareholder on:

Shares held:

Membership ceased:

Draft Wording 10 – Nominee's Declaration of Trust

I, [NAME] of [ADDRESS], hereby declare that the [NUMBER] [ordinary, preference, *etc.*] shares of £1 each in the capital of [NAME OF SUBSIDIARY] Limited which are registered in my name are held by me as nominee for [PARENT COMPANY] Limited [*or* plc] ('the owner') and that I have no beneficial interest whatsoever in the said shares.

Accordingly:

1   I agree to hold the said shares and any dividends or other rights arising therefrom for the exclusive benefit of the owner and to pay or deal with such dividends or rights as the owner may direct.

2   I agree to use all voting rights arising from the said shares in such manner as the owner may direct.

3   I authorise the owner to complete the stock transfer form which I have signed and which relates to such shares in such manner and at such time as the owner may decide and at any time to submit such stock transfer form for registration so that the owner may transfer the said shares to itself (himself) or to such person as it (he) may decide.

Signed as a deed and delivered by me

on [DATE] ....

....
[SIGNATURE]

....
[*Type name of nominee beneath signature*]

in the presence of: ....
[WITNESS'S SIGNATURE]

Name: ....

Address: ....

....

....

Occupation: ....

Note: Within 30 days of signature this document must be sent or taken to an Inland Revenue Stamp Office to have a £5.00 stamp impressed.

Draft Wording 11 – Register of Directors and Secretaries

SECRETARIES

Name: ....

Residential address: ....

DIRECTORS

Name: ....

Former names: ....

Residential address: ....

....

Nationality: ....

Business occupation: ....

Became a director on: ....

Ceased: ....

Date of birth: ....

Other directorships held:

Company	Appointed	Ceased

Name: ....

Former names: ....

Residential address: ....

....

Nationality: ....

Business occupation: ....

Became a director on: ....

Ceased: ....

Date of birth: ....

Other directorships held:

Company	Appointed	Ceased

Draft Wording 12 – Notice of Share Transaction

[DIRECTOR'S ADDRESS]
[DATE]

The Secretary,
∗∗ Limited,
[ADDRESS]

Dear Sir,

Register of Directors' Holdings and Interests

In fulfilment of my obligations under Companies Act 1985, section 324, I have to advise you that when I became a director on [DATE] I held [NUMBER] [ordinary, preference, *etc.*] shares in the company [and/or] I held [NUMBER] [ordinary, preference, *etc.*] shares in the XYZ plc which is this company's holding company.

[*or:*] In fulfilment of my obligations under Companies Act 1985, section 324, I have to advise you that on [DATE] I [bought/sold] [NUMBER] [ordinary, preference, *etc.*] shares in the company for a consideration of £ ——— [COST OR PROCEEDS].

[*or:*] In fulfilment of my obligations under Companies Act 1985, section 324, I have to advise you that on 15 June 1999 my son, John David Smith, became contingently interested in 5,000 10½% cumulative preference shares of £1 each in XYZ plc, this company's ultimate holding company, under the terms of a trust established by his grandmother's will. This contingent interest could only become absolute if several other members of my wife's family were to die before my son reaches the age of 18, and neither I nor my wife nor my son can receive any dividends or deal in any way with the shares in the meantime. I request that the remote nature of this interest be recorded in full in the company's Register of Directors' Holdings and Interests.

Yours faithfully,

. . . .

Note: The first two examples are simple and self-explanatory. The third example is included to show the complexities (and verbosity!) that can and often do arise. In such a case a solicitor will usually have dealt with the will or trust and the director may be well advised to seek his guidance on whether formal notification is required and, if so, in what terms. It would have been useful to record the date of the son's eighteenth birthday (although this is not required by law), so that the secretary may then enquire whether the entry is still necessary.

Draft Wording 13 – Register of Directors' Holdings and Interests

On [DATE] [DIRECTOR'S NAME] notified the company, in fulfilment of his obligations under Companies Act 1985, section 324, that when he became a director on [DATE] he held [NUMBER] [ordinary, preference, *etc.*] shares in the company.

On [DATE] [DIRECTOR'S NAME] notified the company, in fulfilment of his obligations under Companies Act 1985, section 324, that on [DATE] he [bought/sold] [NUMBER] [ordinary, preference, *etc.*] shares in the company for a consideration of £ ____ [COST OR PROCEEDS].

Note: Subject to including (1) the director's name, (2) the date of the transaction, (3) the nature of the transaction, (4) the number of shares, and (5) the consideration, the wording should follow as closely as possible the words used by the director in his formal notification to the company.

Draft Wording 14 – Shareholders' Resolution in Writing

XYZ Limited

SPECIAL RESOLUTION

passed in writing by all the members of the company pursuant to regulation 53 of Table A which forms part of the Articles of Association of this company.

It is hereby resolved that the name of the company be changed to:

ABC Limited

. . . .   (A. B. Black)

. . . .   (C. D. Brown)

. . . .   (E. F. Green)

Dated . . . . 20 . .

Draft Wording 15 – Notice of Meeting, with Waiver

* * Limited

[ADDRESS]

To the (ordinary) shareholders

NOTICE OF MEETING

Notice is hereby given that an extraordinary general meeting of the shareholders of * * Limited will be held at [PLACE] on [DATE] commencing at [TIME] to consider the following which will be proposed as a Special Resolution:

SPECIAL RESOLUTION

That the name of the company be changed to:

ABC Limited

Any member entitled to attend and vote at this meeting may appoint a proxy who need not be a member but who may vote for him on a poll.

By order of the Board,

. . . .
Secretary

WAIVER OF STATUTORY PERIOD OF NOTICE

We, being (all the) members entitled to attend and vote at the above meeting hereby agree to the meeting being held on the day stated notwithstanding that it has been called by shorter notice than that specified in Companies Act 1985.

. . . .
[SIGNATURE]

. . . .
[SIGNATURE]

. . . .
[SIGNATURE]

Draft Wording 16 – Special Resolutions

Change of company name

That the name of the company be changed to * * Limited

Change of objects clause

That clause 3 of the Memorandum of Association of the company (the objects clause) be amended by the deletion of paragraph 3 thereof and the substitution of the following paragraph to be numbered 3:

3 To carry on the trade of _____ [see examples in Draft Wording 3]

Change of articles of association

That the document annexed hereto and signed by all of us be the Articles of Association of the company to the exclusion of the existing Articles of Association.

That the document laid before this meeting and signed for purposes of identification by the chairman thereof be and is hereby adopted as the Articles of Association of the company to the exclusion of the existing Articles of Association.

That regulation [NUMBER] of the Articles of Association of the company shall no longer apply but the following be substituted:

[Insert revised wording here]

That regulation [NUMBER] of Table A shall cease to apply to the company.

That regulation [NUMBER] of Table A shall cease to apply to the company but the following new regulation shall be substituted therefor and numbered [NUMBER] in the Articles of Association of the company:

[Insert revised wording here]

That the Articles of Association of the company be amended by the addition of the following new regulation to be numbered __ [e.g. 29A] and inserted immediately after regulation __ [e.g. 29].

That regulation [NUMBER] of the Articles of Association of the company be deleted and regulations [NUMBER] to [NUMBER] be respectively renumbered [NUMBER] to [NUMBER] inclusive.

Draft Wording 17 – Minutes of Meeting (as notified in Draft Wording 15)

* * Limited

MINUTES
of an extraordinary general meeting of the shareholders
held at [PLACE] on [DATE] commencing at [TIME].

Present: Mr————————— (Chairman)
Mrs ————————— (Director)
Ms————————— (Director)
Mr————————— (Shareholder)
Mrs ————————— (Shareholder)

In attendance: Ms————————— (Secretary)

1 Waiver of notice
The Secretary laid before the meeting [NUMBER] documents by which all the shareholders agreed to the meeting being held this day notwithstanding short notice.

2 Change of name [or: 'Alteration to Articles of Association' etc.]
The chairman proposed as a special resolution:

That the name of the company be changed to: ABC Limited

This was put to the meeting and passed by the majority requisite for a special resolution.
[or: This was voted upon and passed unanimously.]

That concluded the meeting.

Draft Wording 18 – Special Resolution: Layout for Filing

No. _____

COMPANIES ACT 1985

COMPANIES ACT 1989

PRIVATE COMPANY LIMITED BY SHARES

** Limited

At an Annual [*or:* Extraordinary] General Meeting of ** Limited
held on [DATE] at [PLACE] the following resolution was passed as a
Special Resolution:

SPECIAL RESOLUTION

That the name of the company be changed to

ABC Limited

. . . .
[SIGNATURE]

. . . .
[TYPED NAME]

Secretary

Notes:

1 The company number, to be inserted in the top right-hand corner, will be found
on the certificate of incorporation.

2 The exact wording of the resolution, as set out in the notice of the meeting, must
be inserted beneath the words 'SPECIAL RESOLUTION'. Amendments are not
permitted.

Draft Wording 19 – Corporate Shareholder Appointing a Representative

Holding Company Limited

CERTIFIED RESOLUTION

REPRESENTATIVE TO VOTE AS SHAREHOLDER

———————

At a meeting of the board of directors of Holding Company Limited ('the company') held on [DATE] it was resolved:

That the secretary of the company or such other person as may be nominated by the Managing Director of the company be and is hereby appointed the company's representative under section 375 of the Companies Act 1985 to attend and vote for and in the name of the company at any general meeting of members of any other company in which the company holds shares or other securities, with authority to exercise all powers of the company at such meeting or at any adjournment thereof.

———————

Certified a true extract from the minutes of a meeting of the directors of Holding Company Limited held on [DATE OF MEETING].

Signed: . . . .

Secretary of Holding Company Limited

Date: . . . .

Draft Wording 20 – Letter of Request by Personal Representatives

[ADDRESS FOR REPLY]

To the secretary,
∗ ∗ Limited.

LETTER OF REQUEST

We the undersigned, executors of the will [*or:* administrators of the estate] of [NAME OF SHAREHOLDER] deceased, hereby request you to register us in the books of the company as holders of the shares now standing in the name of the deceased.

Signed: ....

Name in full: ....

Address: ....

Signed: ....

Name in full: ....

Address: ....

Date: ....

Note: This Letter of Request must be accompanied by Probate of the Will or Letters of Administration unless the company has already registered that document.

Draft Wording 21 – Stock Transfer Form (front page)

Stock transfer form

[This form to be printed on white paper] STOCK TRANSFER FORM Consideration Money £	Certificate lodged with the Registrar (For completion by the Registrar/ Stock Exchange)

Name of Undertaking	
Description of Security	

Number or amount of Shares, Stock or other security and, in figures column only, number and denomination of units, if any.	Words	Figures
		(units of)

Name(s) of registered holder(s) should be given in full: the address should be given where there is only one holder. If the transfer is not made by the registered holder(s) insert also the name(s) and capacity (e.g., Executor(s)), of the person(s) making the transfer.	in the name(s) of

I/We hereby transfer the above security out of the name(s) aforesaid to the person(s) named below. Signature of transferor(s) 1. .... 3. .... 2. .... 4.	Stamp of Selling Broker(s), for transactions which are not stock exchange transactions, of Agent(s), if any, acting for the Transferor(s). Date

Full name(s), full postal address(es) (including County or, if applicable, Postal District number) of the person(s) to whom the security is transferred. Please state title, if any, or whether Mr, Mrs or Miss. Please complete in type or in Block Capitals.	

I/We request that such entries be made in the register as are necessary to give effect to this transfer.

Stamp of Buying Broker(s) (if any).	Stamp or name and address of person lodging this form (if other than the Buying Broker(s)).

Reference to the Registrar in this form means the registrar or registration agent of the undertaking, not the Registrar of Companies at Companies House.

Draft Wording 21 – Stock Transfer Form (back page)

Form of certificate required for exemption from stamp duty

Instruments of transfer executed on or after 1st May 1987 are exempt from stamp duty when the transaction falls within one of the following categories and will not need to be seen in stamp offices, provided they are certified as below in accordance with the Stamp Duty (Exempt Instruments) Regulations 1987:

(a) The vesting of property subject to a trust in the trustees of the trust on the appointment of a new trustee, or in the continuing trustees on the retirement of a trustee.

(b) The conveyance or transfer of property the subject of a specific devise or legacy to the beneficiary named in the will (or his nominee).

(c) The conveyance or transfer of property which forms part of an intestate's estate to the person entitled on intestacy (or his nominee).

(d) The appropriation of property with Section 84(4) of the Finance Act 1985 (death: appropriation in satisfaction of a general legacy of money) or Section 84(5) or (7) of that Act (death: appropriation in satisfaction of any interest of surviving spouse and in Scotland also of any interest of issue).

(e) The conveyance or transfer of property which forms part of the residuary estate of a testator to a beneficiary(or his no nominee) entitled solely by virtue of his entitlement under the will.

(f) The conveyance or transfer of property out of a settlement in or towards satisfaction of a beneficiary's interest, not being an interest acquired for money or money's worth, being a conveyance or transfer constituting a distribution of property in accordance with the provisions of the settlement.

(g) The conveyance or transfer of property on and in consideration only of marriage to a party to the marriage (or his nominee) or to trustees to be held on the terms of a settlement made in consideration only of the marriage.

(h) The conveyance or transfer of property within Section 83(1) of the Finance Act 1985 (transfers in connection with divorce, etc.)

(i) The conveyance or transfer by the liquidator of property which formed part of the assets of the company in liquidation to a shareholder of that company (or his nominee) in or towards satisfaction of the shareholder's rights on a winding-up.

(j) The grant in fee simple of an easement in or over land for no consideration in money or money's worth.

(k) The grant of a servitude for no consideration in money or money's worth.

(l) The conveyance or transfer of property operating as a voluntary disposition *inter vivos* for no consideration in money or money's worth nor any consideration referred to in Section 57 of the Stamp Act 1891 (conveyance in consideration of a debt, etc.).

(m) The conveyance or transfer of property by an instrument within Section 84(1) of the Finance Act 1985 (death: varying disposition).

Certificate

(1) Insert appropriate category

(2) Delete if the certificate is given by the transferor or his solicitor

I/We hereby certify that this instrument falls within category .... (1) in the schedule to the Stamp Duty (Exempt Instruments) Regulations 1987.
I/We confirm that I/we have been duly authorised by the transferor to sign this certificate and that the facts of the transaction are within my/our knowledge.(2)

Signature(s)..   Description ('Transferor', 'Solicitor' etc)

Name(s) ....

Address ....

Date ....   20 ....

Form of certificate required where transfer is not exempt but is not liable to *ad valorem* stamp duty (£5.00 fixed duty payable)

Some instruments of transfer are liable to a fixed duty of £5.00 when the transaction falls within one of the following categories for which the certificate below may be completed.

(1) Transfer by way of security for a loan or re-transfer to the original transferor on repayment of a loan.

(2) Transfer, not on sale and not arising under any contract of sale and where no beneficial interest in the property passes: (a) to a person who is a mere nominee of, and is nominated only by, the transferor; (b) from a mere nominee who has at all times held the property on behalf of the transferee; (c) from one nominee to another nominee of the same beneficial owner where the first nominee has at all times held the property on behalf of that beneficial owner. (NOTE – This category does not include a transfer made in any of the following circumstances: (i) by a holder of stock, etc., following the grant of an option to purchase the stock, to the person entitled to the option or his nominee; (ii) to a nominee in contemplation of a contract for the sale of stock, etc., then about to be entered into; (iii) from the nominee of a vendor, who has instructed the nominee orally or by some unstamped writing to hold stock, etc., in trust for a purchaser, to such purchaser).

(1) Insert '(1)' or '(2)'

(2) Here set out concisely the facts explaining the transaction in cases falling within (1) or (2) or in any other case where £5.00 fixed duty is offered.

I/We hereby certify that the transaction in respect of which this transfer is made is one which falls within the category .... (1) above.
I/We confirm that I/we have been duly authorised by the transferor to sign this certificate and that the facts of the transaction are within my/our knowledge.

(2)..

....

Signature(s)	*Description ('Transferor', 'Solicitor' etc)*
....	....
....	....
....	....

Date .... 20 .....

Directory

Registrar of Companies – Companies House

CARDIFF
Companies House, Crown Way, Maindy, Cardiff, CF14 3UZ.
Telephone: 029 2038 8588

EDINBURGH
Companies House, 37 Castle Terrace, Edinburgh, EH1 2EB.
Telephone: 0131 535 5800

Much useful information, including a series of Guidance Booklets, is available without charge from the Companies House website: http://www.companies-house.gov.uk

Other Companies House offices:

BIRMINGHAM
Central Library, Chamberlain Square, Birmingham, B3 3HQ.
Telephone: 0121 233 9047

GLASGOW
7 West George Street, Glasgow, G2 1BQ.
Telephone: 0141 221 5513

LEEDS
25 Queen Street, Leeds, LS1 2TW.
Telephone: 0113 233 8338

LONDON
21 Bloomsbury Street, London, WC1B 3XD.
Telephone: 029 2038 0801 (via Cardiff)

MANCHESTER
75 Mosley Street, Manchester, M2 2HR.
Telephone: 0161 236 7500

HM Customs and Excise

For details of your local VAT Advice Centre, refer to your local telephone directory or call 020 7202 4087. A full listing and other useful information are available on the HM Customs and Excise website: http://www.hmce.gov.uk

Home Office Immigration and Nationality Department

Lunar House, Wellesley Road, Croydon, CR9 2BY.
Telephone: 020 8686 0688

Institute of Chartered Secretaries and Administrators

16 Park Crescent, London, W1N 4AH.
Telephone: 020 7580 4741
http://www.icsa.org.uk/icsa/

Institute of Directors

116 Pall Mall, London , SW1Y 5ED.
Telephone: 020 7839 1233
http://www.iod.co.uk

Inland Revenue Stamp Offices

Dorchester House, 52–58 Great Victoria Street, **Belfast**, BT2 7QE.
Telephone: 028 9031 4614

City House, 140–146 Edmund Street, **Birmingham**, B3 2LG.
Telephone: 0121 200 3001

The Pithay, All Saints Street, **Bristol**, BS1 2NY.
Telephone: 0117 927 2022

Companies House, Crown Way, Maindy, **Cardiff**, CF4 3UR.
Telephone: 029 2038 0801

Mulberry House, 16 Picardy Place, **Edinburgh**, EH1 3NF.
Telephone: 0131 556 8511

South West Wing, Bush House, Strand, **London**, WC2B 4QN.
Telephone: 020 7438 7252

Alexandra House, The Parsonage, **Manchester**, M60 9BT.
Telephone: 0161 833 2752

Cale Cross House, 156 Pilgrim Street, **Newcastle-on-Tyne**, NE1 6TF.
Telephone: 0191 245 0200

Room 57, East Block, Barrington Road, **Worthing**, BN12 4SE.
Telephone: 01903 508930

http://www.inlandrevenue.gov.uk

The Stationery Office

16 Arthur Street, **Belfast**, BT1 4GD
Telephone: 028 9023 8451

68–69 Bull Street, **Birmingham**, B4 6AD.
Telephone: 0121 236 9696

33 Wine Street, **Bristol**, BS1 2BQ.
Telephone: 0117 926 4306

TSO Oriel Bookshop, The Friary, **Cardiff**, CF1 4AA.
Telephone: 029 2039 5548

71 Lothian Road, **Edinburgh**, EH3 9AZ.
Telephone: 0131 228 4181

123 Kingsway, **London**, WC2B 6PQ.
Telephone: 020 7242 6393

9–21 Princess Street, **Manchester**, M60 8AS.
Telephone: 0161 834 7201

http://www.tso-online.co.uk

Companies Acts and other government publications are also available through booksellers; the most recent legislation can be downloaded from the HMSO website:
http://www.hmso.gov.uk

Trade Marks Register

Harmsworth House, 13–15 Bouverie Street, **London** EC4Y 8DP.
Concept House, Cardiff Road, **Newport**, South Wales NP10 8QQ.
Telephone: 01633 813930; E-mail: enquiries@patent.gov.uk

Index